AUG - 2005

Greeting Cards Galore

Greeting cards Galore

MICKEY BASKETT
&
MARCI DONLEY

Sterling Publishing Co., Inc.
New York

Prolific Impressions Production Staff:
Editor in Chief: Mickey Baskett
Copy Editor: Phyllis Mueller
Graphics: Dianne Miller, Karen Turpin
Styling: Lenos Key
Photography: Jerry Mucklow
Administration: Jim Baskett

Library of Congress Cataloging-in-Publication Data Available

10 9 8 7 6 5 4 3 2 1

Published by Sterling Publishing Co., Inc.
387 Park Avenue South, New York, N.Y. 10016

© 2005 by Prolific Impressions, Inc.
Produced by Prolific Impressions, Inc.
160 South Candler St., Decatur, GA 30030

Distributed in Canada by Sterling Publishing
c/o Manda Group, 165 Dufferin Street,
Toronto, Ontario, Canada M6K 3H6

Distributed in Great Britain by Chrysalis Books Group PLC, The Chrysalis Building, Bramley Road, London W10 6SP, England

Distributed in Australia by Capricorn Link (Australia) Pty. Ltd.
P.O. Box 704, Windsor, NSW 2756 Australia

Printed in China
Sterling ISBN 1-4027-1470-X

HAPPY·ANNIVERSARY·

Contents

THANK YOU!

HAPPY FATHERS DAY

DAD

ark & animals
B c dove E f
G H i j k L
m noah O P q
rain S T w x y z
U v w x y z

Listen to the Songs Your Heart Sings.

6

Greetings!

That's what this book is about. In these pages, you'll find a wealth of information on making your own greeting cards - cards that express your **best wishes**, cards your friends and family will enjoy receiving, cards the recipients will *cherish as keepsakes*.

You'll learn about the supplies you need and about paper decorating techniques like stenciling, stamping, embossing, collage, and embellishing. You'll get expert tips on crafting *all kinds of cards*, plus professional advice on creating messages and working with photographs.

After learning about the basics, you'll find instructions for more than 45 card projects in a wide array of styles and sizes that were created by talented artists and designers. Some are easy, others are more complicated. All come with color photos, supplies lists, and step-by-step instructions. You can make them just like the designers did or personalize them by adding your own *special touches*.

There are cards for special occasions like birthdays, graduations, weddings, and anniversaries. You'll find birth announcements, valentines, and invitations. There are cards for all kinds of holidays, including Mother's Day, Father's Day, Easter, Christmas, and New Year's, plus cards that express your thanks, extend good wishes, and commemorate special times. *Enjoy making them*, with our best wishes!

Mickey Baskett & Marci Donley

P. S. Handmade cards are often heavier than ones you buy, so if you mail a handmade card, be sure to weigh the card and envelope together and apply the proper postage. You don't want your beautiful creation returned to you with "insufficient postage" stamped on it. When in doubt, visit the post office.

Supplies & Tools
How to Use Them

PAPERS

Papers are the foundation of cards, and there is an infinite selection. As long as you can cut or tear and fold it, any paper can be used to make a card. How you plan to decorate the paper is the main consideration.

Papers also can be used to decorate cards and envelopes and make envelopes. When you mix and match different papers and paper elements, the possibilities are endless.

◼ Purchased Cards

The most convenient way to make a card is to start with a purchased card - a pre-cut blank that usually comes with an envelope. Card blanks come in a huge array of sizes, shapes, colors, textures, and finishes. You can purchase card blanks and envelopes at crafts stores, rubber stamp shops, and stores that sell art supplies and office supplies.

◼ Card & Paper Stock

Print and copy shops have a vast selection of card stock papers that are reasonably priced. Many papers offered by professional printers include matching envelopes. If not, consider purchasing coordinating papers in text (not card) weights to make your envelopes.

A print shop is an excellent source for large sheets of paper, ideal for making accordion-fold or oversized cards. For cards with several layers, consider lighter-weight papers. Most papers carried by print and copy shops are suitable for printing with a laser printer or copier, in addition to stamping and other methods of decorating and lettering. Other sources for papers are art supply stores, rubber stamp shops, and crafts stores.

◼ Handmade Papers

Handmade papers can be used for an entire card or for embellishing. Many contain dried botanicals or other interesting elements. Some are beautifully marbled or silk-screened with a design. They may be more porous or thicker - but not necessarily heavier - than standard card stock. Handmade papers are not recommended for use with laser-printers and copying machines. Try tearing (rather than cutting) the edges of handmade papers to give your card an elegant look.

Handmade papers are available at art, craft and stamp shops or through mail order. They may be offered in stationery-size or wrapping-paper size sheets.

◼ Vellums

Vellums are translucent papers. The most common type is uncolored and offered as card blanks with envelopes. Vellums are versatile and elegant; they should be a basic component of your card-making supplies. Vellum is available in a rainbow of colors, in many printed designs, and embossed.

Vellum can be printed by most laser printers and copiers and stamped or marked with dye-based inks. Vellum accepts acrylic paint very well. Stamping with pigment inks works if you then heat-emboss (otherwise the inks never seem to dry, only to smear.)

Adhesives show through vellum, so if you can't hide your glue with stickers or appliques, punch small decorative shapes from double-sided adhesive to attach vellum at the corners.

Use vellums for wonderful envelopes that showcase your handmade card creations. It's widely available at craft and stamp shops.

◼ Embossed Papers

Embossed papers are an easy way to add texture. Many colors and embossed designs are available at craft and stamp stores. Don't forget embossed handmade papers and wallpapers for special effects.

Printed Papers & Wrapping Paper

A huge variety of decorative papers are readily available. Printed sheets and decoupage papers can be found at crafts and stamping stores. Use the whole sheet or cut out motifs for embellishing.

Sources for decorative papers and wrapping paper include card shops, grocery stores, paper outlets, and gift shops.

Watercolor Paper

Use this heavy-weight paper to make hand painted cards. Find this at art and craft shops.

of your crafts or department store. Here are some suggestions:

• Stardust papers, for backgrounds and accents.
• Decoupage papers, including revivals of lovely vintage prints.
• Tissue paper, in colors, prints, and pearlized finishes. Use double-sided tape or spray adhesives (not wet glue) with tissues for best results.
• Recycled cards, for their images and messages.
• Magazine photos and graphics, as decorative elements. Don't overlook the colorful backgrounds.
• Laser and die-cut elements created for scrapbooking, for framing other elements.

Wallpaper

Wallpaper can be purchased by the roll at home improvement centers and decorating stores. For a variety of smaller pieces, ask for outdated sample books. They contain beautiful papers and usually are free for the asking.

Photocopies

You can create your own colored paper with photos, cut-out images, or other flat objects, such as flowers and leaves, by photocopying them on a color copier. It's a good idea to arrange the images on an 8-1/2" x 11" or 11" x 17" sheet of paper and secure them in place before taking them to a copy shop. Keep in mind that most copiers can reduce and enlarge.

Decorative Specialty Papers

Specialty papers and materials are generally used for decoration and embellishment rather than an entire card. You'll find lots of paper materials for cards in the scrapbooking section

• Paper doilies and foil trims, for elegance and a feminine touch.
• Paper napkins, with their array of images and colors, can be used like other paper motifs - just separate the layers and use only the top printed layer. Treat the printed layer like tissue and use appropriate adhesives.
• Clip art, from books, magazines, or the Internet, can be copied (and enlarged or reduced) on white or colored paper. Add color with markers, paint, or colored pencils.
• Fake fur sheets have a nap and realistic feel.
• Moving images film, available in sheets.
• Metallic and hologram foils and films, for shimmer and sparkle. Many are adhesive-backed; they're also available on rolls. Kids love them.
• Two-tone papers are a different color on each side. Two-tone papers may be card stock or paper weight.
• Velveteen papers add a beautiful look and feel. They can be stamped, although the design will look somewhat muted.

CUTTING & MEASURING TOOLS

A visit to the scrapbooking section of craft stores will reveal many options for cutting and measuring.
Start with a few basics, then add others.

◾ Scissors

A good, **standard-sized scissors** will be your most-used tool. A **small scissors with very sharp points** is indispensable for cutting out small shapes for collage or applique.

Decorative edge scissors or paper edgers are wonderful for adding interesting and elegant edges. The types include pinking, scalloping, and deckle, among others.

◾ Corner Cutters

Corner cutters allow you to make professional-looking rounded or decorative corners on your card and card components.

◾ Craft Knife

The one tool (besides scissors) you must have is a craft knife. A sharp blade is essential - it will cut through card stock or paper with a single stroke and slight pressure. If you find yourself exerting excess pressure or having to re-cut, the blade is dull. Replace it!

◾ Paper Cutters

Paper cutters or paper trimmers, with a sliding or swing-action blade, save lots of time when cutting basic squares and rectangles. Some types have interchangeable rotary blades for creating decorative edges.

◾ Ruler

A metal or metal-edge ruler, at least 12" long (18" is better), is necessary for cutting straight edges with your craft knife. Don't use an inexpensive plastic ruler - the knife will damage it.

A thick, see-through **quilter's ruler** is wonderful for cutting and measuring, but it's a bit more costly. If your budget allows, get a ruler at least 12" long made of 1/4" thick clear acrylic with a right-angle grid - it's ideal for cutting and measuring.

■ Decorative Punches

You can achieve many different looks very quickly with punches, and they're fun to use. Some punch a small shape, usually 1/4" or less. (Be sure to save the punched-out shapes - they make great embellishments.) Larger punches come in a myriad of shapes and designs.

It takes practice to gauge exactly where the punch will occur, so practice on scrap paper before punching your card. Some punches have a longer "reach" so you can punch farther in from the edge of the paper; others allow you to only punch 1/4" or so from the edge.

■ Rotary Cutters

These tools make long, continuous cuts when used with a metal ruler or quilter's straight edge. Interchangeable blades make it possible to cut perforated lines and wavy and other decorative edges, but it's best not to use a straight edge with them.

■ Circle & Oval Cutters

Circle cutters make it possible to cut professional-looking circles. The cutter's adjustable arm can cut (or draw) perfect circles in any size you wish, from 1" to 8" in diameter. A similar tool allows you to draw or cut perfect ovals.

■ Cutting Mat

A self-healing cutting mat protects your work surface and helps extend the life of your blades. Most mats have a measuring grid - a most useful bonus. If you don't have a cutting mat, protect your work surface with heavy chipboard or matte board. Change it often - old cuts can make the knife blade veer off course and ruin a smooth slice.

■ Bone Folder

Bone folders are made of bone and are used to score paper for folding and to press sharp creases. An 8" size is best. Find bone folders at craft and art supply stores.

Scoring with a bone folder.

Creasing with a bone folder.

Paint & Other Coloring Mediums

Paper Paint

Paper paints are designed to work on just about any paper. You can add wonderful color, dimension, and accents to cards with paper paint on just about any type of paper.

The new paper paints are acid free and, when dry, won't stick to other paper surfaces. They are flexible and won't crack as the paper bends, making them perfect for cards that will be mailed, and they don't distort the paper like many paints do.

Dimensional paper paints come in squeeze bottles with applicator tips, so they're easy to use for embellishing and writing. They can be used to create dimensional, textured, or flat finishes. You can thin this paint with a clear medium made specifically for it and use it for brush painting or use more medium and use it like a wash.

Paper paint comes in a variety of opaque colors as well as glitters and metallics. Additionally, there are clear glass-like colors that can be applied over images to give the look of embossing. Follow package directions regarding drying and curing times.

Acrylic Craft Paint

Acrylic paints, generally sold in 2 oz. bottles at crafts stores, are ideal for painted cards. Be aware, however, that the moisture in the paint may cause ripples, buckles, or other distortions to paper. (When the paint dries, the distortion may subside.) Always test acrylic paints on the paper you are using to be sure you will like the results.

Watercolor Paints

Watercolor paints are useful for tinting and achieving a painterly effect. Like acrylics, they may affect some papers adversely, so test first.

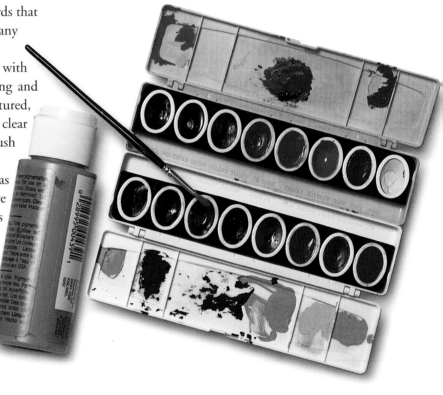

Leafing Pens

Another way to add paint to cards is with **metallic "leafing pens"**. They have a marker-type nib and are filled with lustrous paint in gold, silver, or copper. The ink dries quickly and is super for gilding the edges of cards and envelope flaps.

DIMENSIONAL
Fabric Paint

Colored Pencils

Colored pencils are ideal for use with stamped images and stencils and to enhance painted areas. **Artist-quality colored pencils** and **watercolor pencils** are sold in craft and art supply stores individually and in sets. They are easy to use and the color transfers cleanly and smoothly. You control the intensity by applying light or heavy pressure, and shading and blending is easy.

Brushes

Artist's paint brushes are needed for painted designs and for working with watercolor pencils. Project instructions list the specific brushes you'll need.

Stencil brushes are short-handled brushes especially designed for stenciling. They come in a variety of sizes - the size you use depends on the size of the stencil openings (e.g., small openings require small brushes). Sponge brushes, foam sponges, and sponge-on-a-stick applicators also can be used for stenciling.

Use an old **toothbrush** with diluted paint for spattering (flyspecking).

Markers

Air-erase pens are great for tracing marks and lines on paper - the marks fade away in 24 to 48 hours. Be sure to purchase an air-erase, *not* a water-erase pen when working on paper. Find them in fabric or scrapbooking departments of crafts stores.

Try **colored felt-tip pens**, **calligraphy pens**, **gel pens**, and **paint markers** for decorative treatments and writing. There are also markers made for inking stamps. The array of sizes and colors available is amazing. Find them at crafts, art supply, and office supply stores.

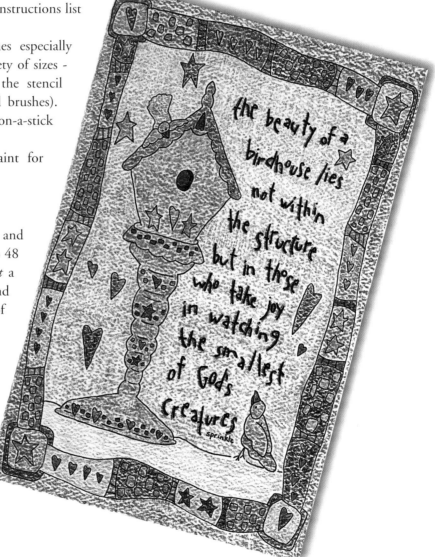

the beauty of a birdhouse lies not within the structure but in those who take joy in watching the smallest of God's creatures

Pictured above: Colored pencils were used in the design of this all-occasion card. Instructions can be found on page 52.

13

RUBBER STAMPS & INKS

Stamped images can be applied to paper with ink, markers, paint, and embossing powders.
Years ago, a rubber stamp was something to mark "Past Due" or "Received" on business
correspondence. There wasn't a whole lot to it - you pressed the stamp on an ink pad and
stamped it on the paper. Today, rubber stamps can turn you into an artist - the only limitation is
your imagination. If you have a sense of color and design, there's no stopping you.
Here are some pointers.

There are different types of stamps. Some are full designs. Some have sentiments or greetings written out for you. There are small stamps and large stamps. There are outline stamps and background stamps. There are factory mounted stamps and unmounted rubber. Each stamp has a purpose, and no one kind is the best.

When you buy stamps, turn over the stamp and look at the rubber. The raised areas hold the ink and make the design, and the recessed areas remain colorless. If your stamp is a leaf, look at the back to determine if what you stamp will be an outline or the full leaf. Both are wonderful, but each produces a different effect. The outline stamp is great if you like to color in the design. The full leaf is great if you want an embossed image.

Learn to look at your stamps as parts. Think of creating your own pictures and scenes with portions of your stamps. For example, if your stamp has a little girl and a teddy bear and you want to stamp only the teddy bear, just ink the part you want. You are not obligated to use the entire image just because it is there. You might find that certain images used with different colors can represent different things. Think outside the box.

Most stamps come as wood mounts - they are more expensive and probably of higher quality, but don't limit yourself. There are wonderful stamps made with heavy foam rubber that do the job as well for a fraction of the price. Some people purchase the rubber and the wood and make their own stamps; another option is to have many unmounted rubber stamps and a few acrylic blocks to use instead of wood.

Choosing Ink

The first ink choice you make is color - you pick what you like. Color availability may determine the ink you choose. But if you find the same color in different inks you have other choices to make - dye ink or pigment ink, large or small pad, raised or flat pad, rainbow or single color, metallic, fabric, waterproof, washable, tattoo, crafter's, petal points, embossing, memory ink - the list goes on.

There are many types of pads and inks. There are a few basic differences, but beyond that, many of the differences are simply brand and design. Some choices cost more. You need more than one ink pad, but you may not need them all.

The most significant difference in pads is the *type of ink.* All pads are either dye or pigment. Dye ink pads contain ink that "drinks" into the paper and dries fairly quickly. Pigment ink pads contain an ink that is thicker, stays on top of the paper, and takes longer to dry. This delay in drying makes pigment ink ideal for heat embossing; however, if you stamp pigment ink on shiny paper or vellum, it will never dry.

Another big difference is the *pad surface.* The first stamp pads were made of compressed fabric set in a frame. They could be re-inked as the pad became dry. These pads are still around, and they are wonderful. They are available in many colors and aren't too expensive, but over time the middle of the pad breaks down and begins to sink, making it difficult to evenly ink a stamp. Also, you can only ink a stamp that is smaller than the frame. To address this, the industry created a raised surface of heavy felt or sponge. Neither breaks down in the middle, and you can easily ink a larger image stamp on the raised pad. Raised surface pads are available in dye and pigment inks. Both are re-inkable, but sometimes it is easier and more economical to get a new pad.

Dye Inks. In the dye ink family there are options. Kids' pads and tattoo inks are both washable. Fabric ink is permanent; once heat set, it will not wash out. Memory ink is longer lasting, fades less, and is acid free. Waterproof ink won't run when used with watercolors or wet markers. There is even scented ink. Though they have different applications, all dye inks are somewhat interchangeable unless you want a particular feature.

Pigment Inks. There are also options in the pigment ink family. Metallic colors add excitement. Watermark colors give an excellent first layer for further stamping. There are dozens of wonderful colors available. Embossing ink is pigment ink that has either no color or a slight tint (but any pigment ink will work for embossing). Embossing ink's main advantage over colored ink is that it is easier to clean off your stamps and it has a slightly longer drying time.

Rainbow pads are available in dye and pigment inks. The colors in a dye ink rainbow pad usually are separated by spacers that you remove when you use the pad - once the barriers are removed, the colors run together. Eventually, you have a pad that does not have clear color separation - not a great investment. The best choice has a little lever that lets you slide the colors together when you want to use the pad and slide them apart before you put it away. Terrific idea, and it works.

Because the ink is thicker, pigment rainbow pads do not run together - they hold their crisp color edges. There are several three- and five-color rainbow pads. A favorite is a round pigment pad with eight different triangles of color. Each triangle is removable, so it's like owning eight different color pads. This is economical and easy to store.

Pads come in different sizes and shapes - traditional rectangles, squares, tiny squares, cat's eyes, huge, tiny, and so on. Some have lids that flip back. (This is nice if you are always searching for the tops.) Little pads give you the option to have many colors at a lower price stored in a smaller space. You can ink a large stamp with a small pad if you turn your stamp (rubber up) and pat the pad over it.

Continued on next page

Stamping with an ink pad.

Inking a stamp with markers.

Another great way to ink a stamp is with markers. Any water-based marker can substitute for a dye ink pad. The markers made for stamping are best because their tips are intended to cover the surface efficiently. Using markers directly on a stamp allows you to produce a multi-colored image, and markers are ideal for traveling stampers.

Caring for Stamps

Be sure to clean your stamps after using them and especially before you ink a stamp with a new color. Clean stamps with water, soap, baby wipes, or stamp cleaner. Don't use products that contain alcohol - it will dry out the rubber. An old washcloth and soft toothbrush are good cleaning supplies.

If you ink a stamp that is already loaded with another color, wipe the surface of the pad with a paper towel. The impression of the other color may be visible, but the excess ink will be gone.

Store your stamps and pads away from sunlight. A handy way to store stamps is to keep them in shallow plastic drawers that are available at discount stores. Pizza boxes are good, too. Do not store ink pads in the refrigerator - they will dry out. Store pads upside down to keep the ink in the top of the stamping surface.

Ink Applicators

A **brayer** is a useful tool for applying ink from a stamp pad to paper to create a colored background. *Interchangeable rollers* will allow you to create large areas of overall patterns.

Another handy ink applicator is the **dauber**. Daubers are small sponges, similar to tiny stamp pads, mounted on pen-size barrels. Many have a different color on each end. They are especially handy for use with small stamps and stenciled areas.

You can use **stencil daubers** to apply ink as well. They are small domed sponges attached to the end of a small dowel and can be used to transfer ink from a stamp pad to paper. Simply tap the sponge end against the stamp pad to load, then tap over a stencil opening to transfer the ink to the paper.

HEAT EMBOSSING SUPPLIES & TOOLS

One of the most dramatic stamping techniques is embossing - the raised, shiny image gives a professional look to your art. Successful embossing depends on three elements working together. The process is like thermographic printing on a (much) smaller scale. It is easy to do once you understand how it works and what supplies to use.

The first element you need is **pigment ink** - you must use pigment ink to stamp your image. (Embossing ink is pigment ink that has no color or just a slight tint. It has a slightly longer drying time and it is easy to clean off your stamps.) Make sure your pad has a good amount of ink on it.

The second element you need is **embossing powder.** Sprinkle the stamped image with embossing powder and it sticks to the wet ink. Embossing powder is made of little bits of plastic, and the size of the bits determines the type of embossing powder. "Detail" embossing powder has fine granules and is designed for use with stamps with fine lines and detail. "Extreme" embossing powders have larger granules for thicker images and sealing wax effects. Unless indicated, most embossing powders are all purpose with medium-size granules.

The third element you need is **heat**. You heat the powder and the powder melts, creating the image. You will get the best results when you use a **heat gun** or **heat tool**. There are many types and all of them work well. They produce a very hot temperature with very little air flow. Some heat guns look like hair dryers, but don't be confused - a hair dryer would remove the powder and not get hot enough. (Heat guns are also used for shrink wrap and paint stripping.)

Here's How to Emboss:
Refer to photos on the next page.
1. Stamp the image with pigment ink.
2. Sprinkle the image with embossing powder.

3. Hold the heat gun above the work and heat the image until all the powder has melted. You can see the color and texture change as it heats. Move the card around slightly to reach the entire image until it is all shiny. At this point, the image will be dry and hot - much like melted wax. Let cool. (And don't touch it until it cools.)

Other Embossing Effects

Embossing pens are available in many colors and tip types, and the ink from just about any ballpoint pen can be used for embossing. (for best results, use an erasable ballpoint pen.) Just write your message, cover with powder, and heat. This is a very impressive way to sign your name.

You can also use embossing powder, ink, and a stamp to produce the look of **sealing wax**. Use pigment ink for the base and sprinkle generously with a heavy embossing powder. Heat until it begins to melt and add more powder while it is hot. Keep melting and adding powder until you have a melted blob. Stamp the hot blob with an inked stamp. Hold the stamp in place until the blob cools, then lift the stamp. You can cut around the impression with a punch or scissors.

To make an **embossed border**, take a two-way glue stick and run it down the edges of the card. Sprinkle with embossing powder and heat. You also can use heat-resistant double-face tape to hold the powder. Find the tape at stamping stores.

EMBOSSING TIPS

- **Work relatively quickly.** Take your time to get the image inked up and placed where you want it, then move right to the next step.
- **You can re-use excess powder.** Always place a sheet of folded paper under your work when you sprinkle the embossing powder. Shake the excess powder off the image and on the paper, then use the paper to pour the excess powder back in the bottle.
- **Colored or clear powder?** The color of the image is determined by the color of the embossing powder, unless you use clear powder - then the ink color determines the color of the embossed image.
- **Custom colors.** Embossing powders can be mixed. (You can find "recipe" books to help you get just the colors you want.) Experiment with small amounts of powders for the desired results.
- **Removing clinging powder.** If, after you pour the powder, you notice powder where you don't want it, brush it away with a soft paint brush or make-up brush. When working on black paper, the powder may stick to the paper and create a snowy effect. To avoid this, use a product you can rub on the paper to reduce the static cling so unwanted powder doesn't stick.
- **Try not to overheat** the powder - if you do, the image will flop, flatten, and burn.

Photo 1. Applying embossing powder to a stamped image.

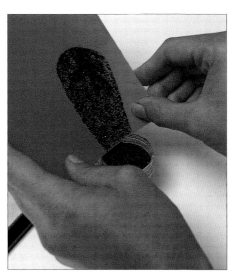

Photo 2. Pouring off excess embossing powder.

Photo 3. Using a heat tool to melt the powder and raise the image.

Stencils

Stenciling is a technique for transferring designs to paper. Acrylic paint, stencil creams or gels, ink from a stamp pad, or colored pencils can be used to apply color through the openings of the stencil. Stencils also can be used to emboss designs.

Types of Stencils

Pre-cut stencils in a huge array of motifs and sizes are available at crafts stores. Stencils for use with paint and ink are generally made of **flexible, transparent plastic; metal stencils** are made specifically for embossing, but just about any stencil can be used to create embossed effects. Test your paper with your stencil to check for compatibility.

Applicators for Stencils

When applying paint, stencil creams or gels, or ink from a stamp pad, choose a stencil brush size that corresponds with the size of the openings of the stencil. To apply larger stenciled images, consider using a stencil roller or a small painter's touch-up roller. You can also use sponge brushes, sponges, and sponge-on-a-stick applicators, which are available in a variety of sizes.

Embossing Tool

The best tool to use for embossing is a stylus with two different end sizes, but just about any stylus with round ball ends can be used for embossing.

Embossing with Stencils

To create a raised effect with a stencil, you work from the back of the paper with the stencil upside down and the paper on top of the stencil. The thicker the stencil material, the deeper (more raised when turned right side up) the embossing will be. *See photos 1 and 2.*

Photo 1. Positioning a stencil for embossing.

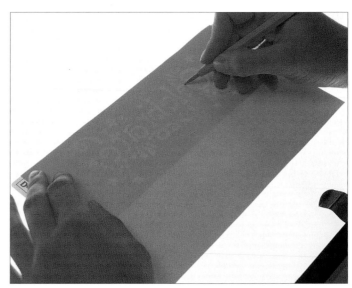

Photo 2. Stencil embossing a transparent paper, using a stylus.

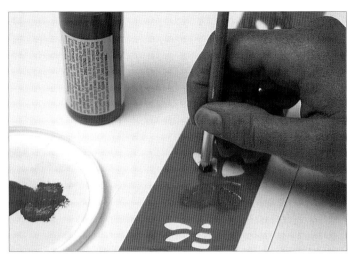

Photo 3. Stenciling with acrylic paint, using a brush.

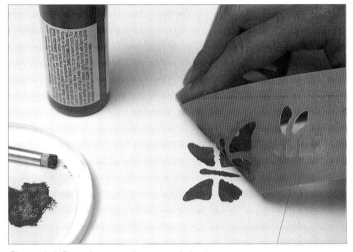

Photo 4. Lifting the stencil to reveal the image.

Photo 5. Stenciling with ink, using a dauber.

Stenciling with Paint

Stenciling is a dry-brush technique - you need very little paint or ink on the brush or other applicator. Dab or swirl the color on the paper through the openings in the stencil. Reload the brush as often as necessary to complete the design. *See photos 3 - 5.*

Stenciling with Colored Pencils

Colored pencils are easy to use with stencils - they don't smear or seep, and they're great for outlining. With pencils, it's also easy to fill in the bridges (the gaps created by the stencil configuration) if you don't want the finished design to look stenciled. *See photo 6.*

Photo 6. Outlining a stencil design with a colored pencil.

Adhesives

You'll need a few different kinds of adhesives, as there's not one universal glue for everything. The best choice varies from one situation to the next, depending on the materials you're using.

■ Double-sided, Dry Adhesives

These are quick and accessible (double-stick tape is one). They may be too bulky for sheer papers, are best for small areas, and come permanent or repositionable. Double-sided sheet adhesives, which have a paper liner on each side, can be cut to any size and shape you need - you peel away the liner from one side and apply it to one surface, then remove the second liner to attach the second surface. Be sure to save and use the small scraps.

Another type of dry adhesive comes in a dispenser and can be rolled on the back of the paper, but it's permanent, so you can't undo a mistake. It's not at all bulky and doesn't show through sheer papers like tissue. (It will show through vellum, however.)

■ Glue Pens & Sticks

Liquid archival glue in a bottle with a small applicator tip (like a marker) is a good choice for small shapes and for sticking paper to paper. It dries fairly quickly, is permanent when dry, and is repositionable while wet. It isn't always strong enough for every kind of applique, and because it soaks in, it doesn't work well on porous surfaces. (Remember if it doesn't hold, you can always use a different adhesive.)

Glue sticks are another handy way to stick things together, especially paper to paper. They work with just about any kind of paper, dry fairly quickly, and are easy to apply.

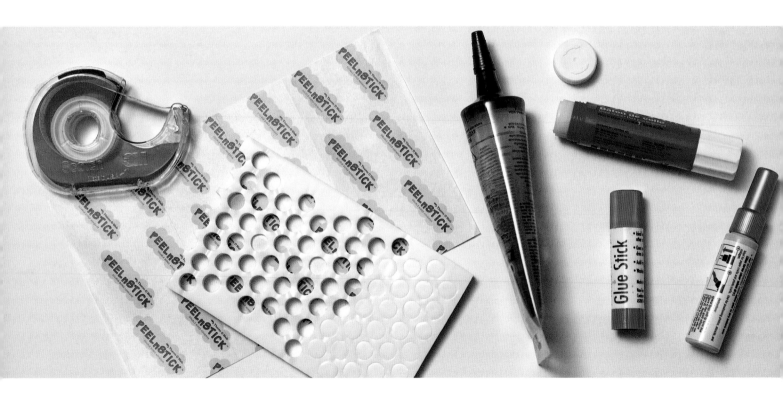

■ Jeweler's Glue

Use jeweler's glue for attaching unusual objects, such as charms, wire, or buttons. Get one that dries clear and sticks to all kinds of surfaces, particularly glass and metal. Use sparingly for best results.

■ Self-Adhesive Foam Circles

These are made of foam and have adhesive on both sides. They give dimension and adhere at the same time. Dimensional dots are generally used for adhering paper to paper, but they can secure lightweight objects. For less dimension, cut double-sided foam carpet tape to size. It's about half as thick as dimensional dots and can be stacked to any height you like.

■ Decoupage Medium

Decoupage medium can be used to glue and apply a protective topcoat to paper. Modern decoupage mediums are brush-on liquids that are clear-drying and non-toxic. You can also find specialty decoupage finishes for antique, pearl, or sepia tones. There's also a decoupage finish that can be used with paint to create a crackled look.

■ Glitter Glue

Glue with glitter suspended in it comes in bottles or in pen-size containers - both with applicator tips so you can write or draw with it.

■ Hot Glue & Glue Sticks

Use this when you need to glue heavier objects to the cards; such as metal charms or buttons.

EMBELLISHING SUPPLIES

■ Beads & Jewels

Small beads (like seed beads) and flat beads (like leaves or other motifs) can add dimension and interest to card designs. Attach them with jeweler's glue or dimensional fabric paint - the applicator tip makes it easy to apply just a tiny dot. When the paint dries, it becomes part of the design; it doesn't have to be "invisible" like other adhesives.

You can also attach beads to cards with thread or wire, or make tassels and strands of beads on thread or wire to attach to cards.

Flat-backed beads and faceted jewels can be glued to cards with jeweler's glue. So can pieces of broken or outdated jewelry.

■ Wire

Wire is available in many colors and can be used as a stand-alone decorative element or as a way to attach other decorations, such as buttons, beads, and charms. Lightweight wire (18 or 24 gauge) is best - you can bend it easily with your fingers. Cut it with round-nose pliers, wire cutters, or needlenose pliers.

■ Charms & Buttons

Charms and buttons can be - well, charming on cards. You'll find a huge selection of motifs at crafts and fabrics stores.

■ Ribbons, Cording, Threads & Yarns

Ribbons, cords, threads, and yarns can be used to add texture, color, sparkle, and movement to cards. You need only small amounts for card decorating, so this is a great way to use small scraps and pieces left from other projects. You'll see many examples in the projects sections.

Special Techniques

This section introduces some special decorating techniques - lettering, collage and layering, and working with photographs. Consider which is going to be the most likely place you might make a mistake, the writing or the painting or stamping, and do that element first. You will feel less pressured as you approach that part of your card-making.

LETTERING

Lettering, used for messages and greetings, is another personal touch you can add to cards. Messages can be created in many ways by many methods. You will soon figure out which ones are most appealing to you and the ones that give you the best results. It is all about personal preference - pick what works and is easiest for you. It doesn't need to be difficult to look great. You want your personal style to shine through. What is easy to you can be impossible for someone else.

To get started, look at cards in card shops to see what types of lettering styles are used. Get a little book just for writing words or sketching styles you can use for your cards. When you see a style of writing you like, make a copy. When you see or hear words that move you, write them down. Whenever something looks good to you, add it to your little book. You will always have ideas to work from.

There are many wonderful pens available - permanent markers, calligraphy pens in a variety of sizes, gel pens, paint pens, markers in all colors and tips, tiny-tip pens, heavy tipped pens and so on. Have a variety of styles and colors available so you can coordinate colors and styles to your designs.

Sometimes your own handwriting is the most meaningful way to convey your personal message. It doesn't have to be picture perfect to be wonderful. If you are going to write a message directly on the card, practice first on scratch paper to work out the placement, spacing, and size of the lettering. Test the pen to be sure it doesn't bleed, is the right color, and looks good on the paper; then use a light box and trace the message on the card or write the message lightly in pencil before inking. Good preparation helps you avoid spelling, spacing, and wiggly line errors. When the ink is thoroughly dry, erase your lines with a white eraser.

You can learn calligraphy from a book by following the pictures and directions, but taking a class helps jump start the learning process, teaches the basics, and helps you to avoid bad habits. To become skilled, you must practice, practice, practice! The most formal way to do calligraphy with real ink and steel-nib pens, but markers are an alternative.

Vellum makes it extremely easy to add a message since you can see right through the paper. You can work out the lettering and trace the final version on the vellum, or you can trace just about any lettering you find and add it to your cards.

There are many wonderful and whimsical fonts available on your computer. It is easy to compose your message on the computer and print it out. If you are proficient on the computer you can print it right on the card. If you are using a collage technique you can print out your message and glue it where you want it. You can print it on a piece of nice paper and use that paper as an insert to the card, held in place with a pretty ribbon tie.

You can also print a message on a transparency and lay that on the card. (You'll have a shiny surface and a fun layer.) When you are using a computer you also have the ability to take the printout to a copy machine and enlarge or shrink it, and you can move the words around by cutting and pasting.

Other ways to get words on cards include stencils, press-on letters, stamps, and stickers in many styles. Use stencils with rubber stamp ink pads, or with paint as you would any stenciling project. As with the writing, test your lettering on scratch paper to make sure the layout and spacing works. Don't forget type from magazines and newspapers - you can even create messages "ransom style."

When you are adding lettering with stamps, you can use a stamp positioner to align your letters perfectly, or you can stamp them freely for a bouncy look. Adding little swirls and dots helps to tie the letters together and gives a whimsical feel.

If your lettering doesn't come out perfectly spaced don't scrap the project. You can add dots or pick up a design element from the card to fill up the space and pull the letters together. Glitter is a wonderful fix for many mistakes!

COLLAGE & LAYERING

Collage is an artistic composition of materials and objects on a surface. Many cards in this book are collages - some very basic, some more complex. Layering is a type of collage that uses layers of paper for a decorative effect. All the layers are visible when the final layer is placed; most often the layers form borders of "frames" for the layer that follows.

A card collage might be layers of papers or might start with papers and include charms, old postage stamps, buttons, wire, ticket stubs, or flattened bottle caps. There are no limits and no rules.

Use adhesives that are appropriate for the elements in your collage - you may need to use several types at different stages of your composition.

Supplies for Collages

Any or all may be incorporated.
• Papers for color and shape
• Paper images (clip art, stamped images, photos, magazine clips, stickers, parts of other greeting cards)
• Paper ephemera (ticket stubs, birth announcements, baseball cards, postage stamps or color photocopies of any of these)
• Three-dimensional materials (dried botanicals, miniatures, ribbons, wire, beads, charms, buttons, feathers, stickers)
• Adhesives

Basic Collage Method

1. Start with a card foundation. Lay out your materials and try different arrangements until you find one you like. It doesn't have to be exact at this point - you are just deciding what to include and what to save for another project.
2. Build your collage layer by layer, using adhesives appropriate to each connection. Try to avoid adding bulk, but ensure the adhesion between the layers is strong enough to hold as successive layers are added. If necessary, set aside so each layer can dry before proceeding to the next.

Basic Layering Method

1. Start with a card foundation. Try different combinations of papers until you arrive at an arrangement that pleases you.
2. Cut out the papers, making each successive layer smaller that the preceding one.
3. Glue the layers, using adhesives appropriate to each connection. Ensure the adhesion between the layers is strong enough to hold as successive layers are added. If necessary, set aside so each layer can dry before proceeding to the next.

WORKING WITH PHOTOGRAPHS

It's nice to send photographs with cards, and even nicer to make the photo part of the card. Photocopies of your photographs or computer printouts of digital or scanned photos are not as bulky as photos, and they last longer. But if, for example, you are planning to send the same photo to many people at the same time (like a family photo at Christmas time or a birth announcement), the most economical and timesaving option may be to have the photo duplicated. Another option is to use a photo printer, if your photo is digital.

Photocopying Tips

- The best way to copy photos is on a color copier - even black and white photos look better when copied in color. Some copiers can copy your photos in a sepia tone, which gives them an old-time feel.
- If you have the time and the funds, copy the photos in a few different sizes. Most copiers use 8-1/2" x 11" or 8-1/2" x 14" paper; take advantage of the size and copy more than one photo on each sheet. Then when you get to creating you will have lots of photos and sizes to pick from.
- Visit the copy store when it's not crowded. You'll have better luck getting the results you want. Many operators are glad to help if they don't have lots of customers waiting in line.

Frame Cards

The simplest way to show your photos is to attach them to a pre-made photo card that has a place for the photo and a built-in border. You can turn a simple photo into a framed picture just by giving it a photo card. There are different types of photo cards with choices in borders - embossed, decorative cut edges, edges with color, etc.

Look for a frame card that looks good with your photo. Then decide what colors look good with your photo. Is there a design element in the photo that you can use on the frame? There are many ways to add your own touches.

- Rubber stamps are a good place to start. Choose stamps with small images and make a border with them. Or pick a large background stamp and create an all-over design. Or try a combination.

- Use pens or dimensional paints to make dots, swirls, and lines around the photo.

- Glue pieces of decorative paper or add beads, buttons, or even puzzle pieces around the frame.

- Use pressed flowers, silk flowers, or appliques.

- Use a corner punch. The simplest is a corner rounder. There are punches that give your corners many different looks and punches that you use on a separate paper that will make a decorative slot to slip your photo into.

- Trim the photo or cut the frame with decorative edge scissors.

But don't get so carried away that the photo gets lost. Sometimes simple is best. It is easier to make a frame for a specific photo than to make a great frame and hunt down a photo to go in it.

Photo Collage

If just one picture won't do, a collage may be just the thing. Decide what pictures you want to use and put them in front of you, then cut away the parts you want to use. (TIP: Leave a little edge around the desired design to help pop it out.) Try to arrange them in a shape, fitting the pieces together like a puzzle, and mount them on colored card stock. Or mount the pieces separately on colored paper. Remember you don't have to limit your collage to the photos - add little bits of colored paper, glitter, buttons, beads, or memorabilia.

When you have a creation you like, photocopy it before you send it. That way, you can send it to more than one person.

Photo Transfers

Photo transfers require practice, but the results are unique and special. A transferred photo looks more like a painting than a photo and has an old-time, worn look. You can transfer both black-and-white or color photos or a photocopy of anything you want to transfer.

What You Need:
• Photocopy of the photo or image you wish to transfer
• Paper (90 lb. hot press watercolor paper works great.)
• Acetone and a small rag or cotton balls *or* a blending pen (the kind made to use with markers)
• Burnishing tool

Here's how:
With acetone and cotton balls
1. Working in a well-ventilated area or outdoors, place your copy, face down, on the watercolor paper.

2. Wet a cotton ball or rag with acetone. Rub it on the back of the copy, using pressure when you rub. The acetone should wet the paper enough that you see the difference between wet and dry areas, but it should not run.
3. Work a section at a time, adding more acetone as needed. Occasionally lift a corner of the copy to see if the image is transferring.
4. When the paper is all wet, switch to the burnishing tool and rub until the transfer is complete.

With a blender pen:
Place the copy face down on the watercolor paper. Use the tip of the blender to rub the back of the copy - you will need to exert some pressure. Work one section at a time until the copy transfers to the watercolor paper. If your blender seems to dry out, dip it in acetone and keep rubbing.

You can give black and white transferred images the look of a painted photograph by adding color with pencils, watercolors, photo markers, or chalks. Keep the colors muted for a soft look - adding just a few dabs of color can create a dramatic effect.

When you have transferred the image, you can:
• Mount it on a card directly
• Mount it on a colored background and then the card
• Trim it with decorative scissors or tear the edges, then mount it

You also can transfer the image to a piece of paper that's large enough to be the whole card. Add words to the image in your own handwriting, with stamped letters, or with a printed caption.

Birthday Cards

What could be more special for someone's special day than a handmade card? This section contains a variety of cards suitable for all ages, including the young and the young-at-heart.

Happy Birthday Times Three

By Marci Donley

This simple-to-make card is decorated with paper tags from an office supply store. You can make your own tags, if you prefer - cut a rectangle the size you want, cut off two of the corners, and punch a hole. It is very easy and economical. If you like, use white or colored reinforcements around the holes.

SUPPLIES

Paper:

White coated card stock, 4-1/2" x 11"

Black medium tag

4 small tags in neon greens

Tools & Other Supplies:

Small message rubber stamps - Happy Birthday, Celebrate

Pigment ink - Black

Embossing powder - Clear

12" sheer black ribbon, 3/4" wide

White string

Self-adhesive foam circles

Glue

Fine-tip black marker

INSTRUCTIONS

1. Score and fold the card stock to make a card 5-1/2" x 4-1/2".

2. Stamp three small tags with the Happy Birthday stamp and black pigment ink. Stamp one small tag with "Celebrate." Emboss with clear powder.

3. Using the black tag as a template, draw a tag on the front of the envelope. Write "TO:" and draw lines with a black pen.

4. Loop the black ribbon through the hole in the black tag.

5. Tie string through the holes of the small tags. (Shorten the strings that come with the tags.)

6. Glue the black tag to the front of the card.

7. Use foam circles to secure the three small "Happy Birthday" tags to the black tag. Use a foam circle to secure the "Celebrate" tag inside the card. ❑

Birthday Accordion Card

By Marci Donley

I have found that sequin waste ribbon (the kind that has rows of holes cut out of it) can be a terrific stencil for creating textured backgrounds. You could also use netting or other textured fabrics or plastics.

Matboard glued to first panel

Matboard glued to last panel

Accordion folds

SUPPLIES

Paper:

2 pieces mat board, each 4" x 4"

2 pieces hand-made paper, 5" x 5"

Good quality parchment-colored writing paper, 15" x 3-3/4"

Vellum, 10" x 10" for making envelope

Tools & Other Supplies:

Sequin waste ribbon, 3-1/4" wide, to use as a stencil

Sponge brush *or* stencil brush

12" purple grosgrain ribbon, 3/4" or 1" wide

Stamps - Happy Birthday, flower, border dot

Stamp ink squares - Blue, gold

Cat's eye ink pads - Green, purple

Black marker, .8

Charm or button, 1-1/4" (To make a charm, see the instructions that follow.)

Glue

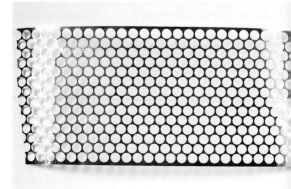

Sequin waste ribbon used as a stencil

Card folded and secured with ribbon band

Envelope made from vellum

INSTRUCTIONS

1. Glue the hand-made paper squares to one side of each piece of mat board, covering all the edges and making sure both sides are smooth.
2. Fold the writing paper in half, and then fold each end into the center fold. (You should have four squares in an accordion fold.)
3. Use the sequin ribbon "stencil" with the green, purple, and gold inks to create a background on one side of the folded paper. Don't worry about matching the pattern, and keep the color light.
4. Using the blue stamp square, lightly stamp a row of diamonds across the middle of the paper.
5. Stamp "Happy Birthday" on one section of the paper, being careful not to have the stamp cross a fold.
6. Stamp a dot border across the paper, skipping over "Happy Birthday."
7. Stamp the flower, placing one on the first square and a few more on the third and fourth squares. Once again, avoid the folds.
8. Use the green cat's eye ink pad to stamp the leaves.
9. With the black marker, outline the flowers, leaves, and "Happy Birthday." TIP: Let your outline be free and loose to give life to the design. Practice on a sheet of scrap paper. (Your practice piece may become another work of art!)
10. Glue the back sides of the covered matboard squares to the back of the front and last panel of the decorated writing paper.
11. Wrap the ribbon around the folded card. Stitch or glue so it can slide on and off.
12. Glue a charm or button on the ribbon where the ends overlap.
13. Make an envelope frm the vellum. ❏

MAKING A CHARM

You'll Need:
A small round stamp design
A large round hole punch
Pigment ink
Copper embossing powder
Card stock
Embossing heat tool

Here's How
1. Rub some pigment ink on a piece of card stock in an area about 2" square.
2. Pour some copper embossing powder on this ink and heat. Add more embossing powder and melt it - about three additions should do it.
3. When the powder is melted, press a pre-inked stamp in the powder. Hold the stamp in place until the powder cools.
4. When the charm is cool and firm, punch out the charm. ❏

Black & White Birthday Tag

By Marci Donley

SUPPLIES

Paper:

White card stock, 8-1/2" x 11"

Black card stock, 8-1/2" x 5-1/2"

Black business-size envelope

Tools & Other Supplies:

Stamps - Deco background,
    deco border

Memory ink pad - Black

Hole punch

13"-16" of three types of ribbon,
    various widths, colors, and textures

Self-adhesive foam circles

Craft knife

Computer and printer

30

INSTRUCTIONS

MAKE THE TAGS

1. Cut the white card stock to 8-1/2" x 3-3/4". Mark the center of the top and cut the corners to make it look like a tag. (I came in 3/4" on the top and sides and cut from one mark to the other.)
2. Punch a hole in the center top.
3. Mark the center of the long edge of the black card stock. Measure 1-1/2" in both directions from that point. Score and fold to make a tri-fold card.
4. Cut the corners off one end of the folded black card so it looks like a tag. Cut a slit in the other end for a closure.

STAMP

1. Stamp the white tag with black ink, using a background stamp. But be sure to stamp all the way to the edges.
2. Stamp three border sections on leftover white card stock. Cut out and set aside.

ASSEMBLE

1. Create a greeting for the inside of the folded black card on the computer. Cut to fit. Glue in place.
2. Glue one stamped border piece on the inside and one on the outside of the black card. Glue the third on the envelope.
3. Secure the back card to the white tag with foam circles.
4. Loop and tie the ribbons through the hole in the tag. ❑

Simply Happy Birthday

By Marci Donley

SUPPLIES

Paper:

Black photo frame card and envelope, 5" x 7"

Green vellum, 4" x 6"

Tools & Other Supplies:

Stamps - Background design, large Happy Birthday

Pigment ink - Black

Embossing powders - Clear, gold

Small black grommets & grommet setting tools

INSTRUCTIONS

1. Stamp the background stamp on the face of the card on the area within the frame. Emboss with gold powder. (This doesn't have to be perfect - since you are going to cover it, you only need a ghost of the stamp for texture.)

2. Trim the vellum to fit inside the frame.

3. Stamp Happy Birthday on the vellum with black ink. Emboss with clear powder.

4. Attach the vellum to the face of the card with grommets, placing a grommet in each corner. ❏

Happy Birthday, Sweet Girl

By Marci Donley

See page 34 for instructions.

Happy Birthday, Sweet Girl

Pictured on page 33

SUPPLIES

Paper:

Foam core board, 4" x 5-3/4"

White envelope, 4-1/4" x 6-1/2"

White card stock or art paper,
   12-1/2" x 6"

Purple accent paper

2 pieces acetate transparency,
   each 3-7/8" x 5-5/8"

Tools & Other Supplies:

Stamps - "Happy Birthday," "Sweet,"
   "Girl," plus letter stamps for a
   greeting

Ink pads - Eggplant, off-white

White embossing powder

Treasures (Beads, small charms,
   confetti, colored wire, glitter)

Craft knife

Glue

Double-sided tape

INSTRUCTIONS

MAKE THE WINDOW

1. Use the pattern provided to cut the card stock.
2. Place the foam core board on the center panel of card and mark the area of the foam board to be cut out. Make the cutout area slightly larger (about 1/8") than the cutout on the card so the edges will be hidden. You will make a window through the card and the foam board.
3. On one side of the foam core board apply double-sided tape around the edges of the window. Apply more around the first tape.
4. Press one piece of acetate over the window and press the edges to secure. (This ensures your treasure will stay within the window.)
5. Add the treasures to the window, setting aside a few pieces of confetti. Test to be sure you have the desired effect.
6. Using more double-sided tape, attach the second piece of acetate to the other side of the foam core board over window.
7. Place the foam core piece on the center panel of the card and secure with double-sided tape.
8. Fold the top panel of the card down over the foam core, lining up the cutouts, and secure in place with double-sided tape.

DECORATE

1. Cut a frame for the window from purple paper.
2. Stamp a message on the frame with off-white pigment ink and emboss. Stamp additional messages on strips of purple paper and emboss. Glue to the front of the card and to the envelope.
3. Stamp a message inside the card with eggplant ink.
4. Glue some confetti inside the card. ❑

Happy Birthday, Sweet Girl
PATTERN

Enlarge @140% for actual size.

Cut on the solid lines.
Score and fold on
the broken lines.

This panel folds down and
glues to foam core

Score

Foam core glued to
inside of this panel

Score

Inside of Back Panel

Birthday Balloons
PATTERNS
(Actual size)

Instructions begin on page 36.

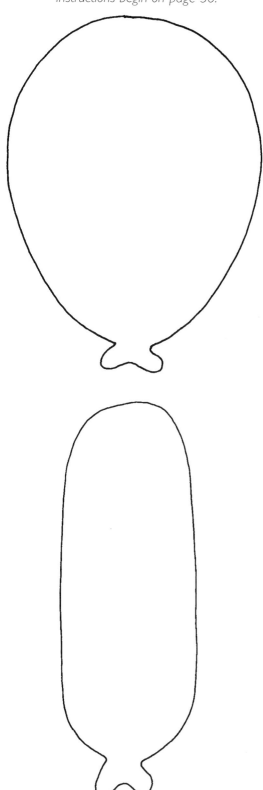

Birthday Balloons

By Marci Donley

SUPPLIES

Paper:

Off-white card and envelope, 5" x 7"

Dimensional Paper Paint:

Yellow

White

Light blue

Black

Tools & Other Supplies:

Craft foam - Red, green, blue, yellow, die cut into balloon shapes

Black embroidery thread *or* thin string

Ink pads - Multi-color, waterproof black

Sponge

Markers - Orange, pink, yellow

Stamps - Tiger motif, swirl lower case alphabet

Stencil/template - Cloud and grass

Self-adhesive foam circles

Craft knife

Patterns on page 35

Patterns on page 35

INSTRUCTIONS

1. On the card front, use the stencil/template with ink (blue for the clouds, green for the grass) to sponge the grass and clouds.

2. Stamp the tiger on the card front with black ink. Color with markers.

3. Tie a black thread to each balloon shape.

4. Decorate the balloons with dimensional paint. Set aside to dry.

5. Stamp a message inside the card, using many ink colors. Put a Black dot of paint between each letter.

6. Use a craft knife to cut small slits around the tiger's paw. Push the threads through the slits so it looks like the tiger is holding the balloons.

7. Secure the balloons to the card front with foam circles.

8. Secure a balloon inside the card to hide the back of the tiger's hand.

9. *Option:* If you're not mailing the card, attach a balloon to the envelope. Add a string and glue in place. Write the recipient's name on the balloon. ❑

Stylish Birthday

By Marci Donley

Here's a card design for your shoe-loving friends. I used a sheet of wrapping paper with lots of shoes, flowers, and bags. Look for designs in magazines, catalogs, old books, or printed gift wrap or decoupage paper.

SUPPLIES

Paper:

Yellow art paper, 18" x 4"

Motifs cut from paper

1 transparency sheet for copier or printer

Black envelope, 9-1/2" x 4-1/8"

Tools & Other Supplies:

Computer & printer

Double-sided tape

Multi-color boucle yarn

Antique decoupage medium

Red foil tape, 1/8" wide

It's Your Birthday........
Step Out in Style!

INSTRUCTIONS

DECOUPAGE

1. Score and fold the paper to create a card 9" x 4".

2. Arrange paper cutouts on the card front and inside the card. Adhere with decoupage medium. Let dry.

3. Brush a coat of decoupage medium over the front of the card. Let dry. Brush a coat of decoupage medium over the cutouts on the inside. Let dry.

4. Adhere a cutout to one corner of the envelope.

ASSEMBLE

1. Trim the edges of the card with red foil tape.

2. Use your computer to print a message on plain paper (this one is "It's Your Birthday..... Step Out in Style") in a font that looks good with the design. Hold the printout over the card to check the placement. When you are satisfied with the font and placement, proceed to the next step.

3. *Option 1:* Print out the message on colored paper. Cut out the message and glue one part to front and one part of message to inside. *Option 2:* Print each part of the message on a transparent sheet that is cut large enough to cover front and inside, plus enough for a fold over. (Cut each piece of transparent sheet to 9-1/4" x 4" which is the size of the card plus 1/4".)

4. Position the message on the front of the card, folding the extra 1/4" over the left edge. Secure in place with double-sided tape.

5. Position the inside message, folding the extra 1/4" over the right side to the back. Secure in place with double-sided tape.

6. Tie the yarn around the fold and knot. Tie on additional pieces of yard to make a tassel. ❑

39

Cards for Any Occasion

Sending a card is great way to keep in touch or share a thought, an idea, or a photo. These cards can be sent instead of a gift or as a gift, and some of them include a gift. They represent a variety of styles and media - some are collages; others are colored with watercolor pencils or paint.

Sisters - Then & Now

By Marci Donley

To make this card, I chose photos and photo motif stamps with a sisters theme. You might choose kids, moms, family, or a vacation or other fun event.

Instructions begin on page 42.

SUPPLIES

Paper:

White card stock, 6" x 12", plus scraps

Black decorative paper with white highlights

Vellum, 4" square

Photos copied in black and white

Dimensional Paper Paint:

Black

Tapioca

Tools & Other Supplies:

Decorative edge ruler

Stamps - Woven background, 2 with photo motifs

Memory ink pad - Black

2 black skeletal leaves

2 round tags with white tie strings

Butterfly stickers

Canceled postage stamp

Glue

Fine-tip permanent marker - Black

41

Sisters - Then & Now
continued from page 41

INSTRUCTIONS

FOLD, TEAR & STAMP

1. Fold white card in half to make a 6" square card.

2. Tear the black decorative paper using a decorative edge ruler so the paper is just slightly smaller than the front of the card.

3. Stamp the photo stamps with black ink on scraps of white card stock.

Tear the edges, using the decorative edge ruler.

4. Stamp the woven background stamp in black on the vellum.

5. Tear some images from the photo-copied photos.

ASSEMBLE & PAINT

1. Arrange the photos, the stamps, and the stamped vellum in a pleasing design. Place some images on top of the vellum and some behind it to create depth.

2. Glue the skeletal leaves on top of the vellum for further depth.

3. Adhere the butterfly stickers and the canceled stamp.

4. Use black paper paint to write the theme (here, "sisters") across the card.

5. Outline the photos with the tapioca paper paint.

6. Write "then" and "now" on the little round tags. Tie the string on each one in a bow. Glue them to the card. ❏

Heart Songs

By Marnie Lyn Adams

SUPPLIES

Paper:

140 lb. cold press watercolor paper, 8-1/2" x 11"

Tools & Other Supplies:

Watercolor pencil - Violet

Black permanent ink pens - 03, 05, 08

Paint brushes - #2 round, #6 round

Graphite transfer paper & stylus

Kneaded eraser

Pencil & sharpener

Ruler

Paper towels

Water container

Tracing paper

INSTRUCTIONS

PREPARE

1. Fold watercolor paper to create a vertical card, 5-1/2" x 8-1/2".

2. Trace pattern. Using graphite paper, transfer pattern to front of card. Use kneaded eraser to erase any mistakes.

COLOR THE DESIGN

See the project photo.

1. Using the violet pencil, color the center section with light pressure, leaving the hearts white.

2. Using the violet pencil, color the outside border with medium pressure, leaving the hearts white.

3. Using the violet pencil, color the large heart and stripes on the inner border with heavy pressure.

4. Wet colored areas, using a brush dampened with water. Use a #6 brush for larger areas and a #2 brush for smaller spaces and around the hearts. Allow to dry overnight. TIP: Every time you put the brush in water, blot it on a paper towel.

INK THE DESIGN

1. Using the 03 pen, ink the thin lines in the inner border and the small hearts.

2. Using the 05 pen, ink the lettering and dots.

3. Using the 08 pen, ink the large heart, thick lines, and shading on large heart and center hearts. ❏

A star is a DREAM waiting to be followed.

sprinklz

*Instructions for
"Star Dream"
begin on
page 46.*

Star Dream

By Marnie Lyn Adams

SUPPLIES

Paper:

140 lb. cold press watercolor paper,
8-1/2" x 11"

Tools & Other Supplies:

Watercolor Pencil - Ultramarine

Black permanent ink pens - 03, 05, 08

Paint brushes - #2 round, #6 round

Graphite transfer paper

Kneaded eraser

Pencil & sharpener

Ruler

Paper towels

Water container

Tracing paper

Pattern on page 45

INSTRUCTIONS

PREPARE

1. Fold the watercolor paper to create a vertical card 5-1/2" x 8-1/2".

2. Trace pattern. Using graphite paper, transfer pattern to front of card. Use kneaded eraser to erase any mistakes.

COLOR

With the ultramarine pencil, using the photo as a guide.

1. Color the center section with light pressure (but leave the stars and moon white).

2. Color the outside border with medium pressure (but leave the stars white).

3. Color the large star and the large sections in the inner border with heavy pressure.

BRUSH

Wet colored areas with a brush dampened with water. Use the #6 brush for larger areas and the #2 brush for small spaces around the stars. Allow to dry overnight. TIP: Every time you out the brush in water, blot it on a paper towel.

INK

1. Using the 03 pen, ink the thin lines in the inner border and the small stars and moon.

2. Using the 05 pen, ink the lettering and dots.

3. Using the 08 pen, ink the large star, the thick lines, and the shading on the large star, moon, and center stars. ❏

A star is a DREAM waiting to be followed.
sprinklz

Roses Tickle Noses

By Marnie Lyn Adams

SUPPLIES

Paper:

140 lb. cold press watercolor paper,
8-1/2" x 11"

Tools & Other Supplies:

Watercolor pencil - Crimson red

Black permanent ink pens - 03, 05, 08

Paint brushes - #2 round, #6 round

Graphite transfer paper

Kneaded eraser

Pencil & sharpener

Ruler

Paper towels

Water container

Tracing paper

See pattern on page 50

INSTRUCTIONS

PREPARE

1. Fold the watercolor paper to create a vertical card 5-1/2" x 8-1/2".

2. Trace pattern. Using graphite paper, transfer pattern to front of card. Use kneaded eraser to erase any mistakes.

COLOR THE DESIGN

Use the crimson red pencil to color and the photo as a guide.

1. Color the center section with light pressure (but leave the roses white).

2. Color the outside border with medium pressure (but leave the roses white).

3. Color the large rose and the inner border squares with heavy pressure, leaving every other square white.

BRUSH & INK

1. Wet colored areas using a brush dampened with water. Use a #6 brush for larger areas, and a #2 brush for small spaces around the roses. Allow to dry overnight. TIP: Every time you put the brush in water, blot it on a paper towel.

2. Using the 03 pen, ink the thin lines in the inner border and the small roses.

3. Using the 05 pen, ink the lettering and dots.

4. Using the 08 pen, ink the large rose, the thick lines, and the shading outlines on the large rose and center roses. ❏

How glorious a treat to be surrounded by roses,

For wondrous their scent That tickles our noses.

sprinklz

How glorious a treat

to be surrounded by roses,

For wondrous their scent

That tickles our noses.
-sprinklz

Beauty of a Birdhouse
PATTERN (actual size)

the beauty of a
birdhouse lies
not within
the structure
but in those
who take joy
in watching
the smallest
of God's
creatures
sprinklz

Instructions begin on page 52.

Beauty of a Birdhouse

By Marnie Lyn Adams

SUPPLIES

Paper:

140 lb. cold press watercolor paper, 8-1/2" x 11"

Colored Pencils:

Canary yellow

Sunburst yellow

Carmine red

Crimson red

True green

Grass green

Non-repro blue

True blue

Tools & Other Supplies:

Black permanent ink pens - 05, 08

Graphite transfer paper

Kneaded eraser

Pencil & sharpener

Ruler

Paper towels

Water container

Tracing paper

INSTRUCTIONS

PREPARE

1. Fold the watercolor paper to create a vertical card 5-1/2" x 8-1/2".

2. Trace pattern. Using graphite paper, transfer pattern to front of card. Use kneaded eraser to erase any mistakes.

INK

1. Using 08 pen, ink the lettering.

2. Using 05 pen, ink the remainder of the lines.

COLOR THE DESIGN

Use the project photo as a guide or use the colors of your choice. ❏

Dots & Cherries Photo Card

By Marci Donley

SUPPLIES

Paper:

White card stock, 6" x 12-1/2"

Photograph or color copy of photograph, 3-3/4" x 5"

Glossy white card stock

Red card stock

Tools & Other Supplies:

Red marker

Stamp - Cherries motif

Ink pad - Black

10" red polka dot wire-edge ribbon, 1-1/2"

Dimensional paper paint - Red, green

Circle punches, 1", 1-1/4"

Ruler

Decorative edge scissors

Glue

This frame card holds a photograph. The thing to remember about frame cards is that the frame should enhance the photograph or at the very least not compete with it. Look at your photo and try to coordinate a color or an image to make your photo look the best it can look. On this frame, I used the cherry design from the little girl's dress as accents.

INSTRUCTIONS

FOLD & CUT

1. Measure, score and fold the long piece of card at 4-1/2" and 8-1/2" to form a three-panel card. The middle panel is for the photo. The first panel folds back to provide a backing for the photo, and the third panel is the inside of the back of the card.

2. Measure and cut an opening in the middle section that is large enough for your photo. (What's left of that section is the frame.)

DECORATE

1. Use the red marker to create a dot pattern on the frame and the envelope flap.

2. Stamp the cherries four times with black ink on glossy white card stock.

3. Use dimensional paints to color the cherries and leaves. Let dry.

4. Punch out the cherries motifs with a 1" circle punch.

5. Punch out four red circles with a 1-1/4" punch. Glue the punched-out cherries to the red circles.

6. Glue the photo in the frame.

7. Tie a ribbon bow and glue to the frame. Glue three cherries punch-outs to the frame as shown. Use the fourth as a seal for the envelope. ❑

Maple Leaf Pin & Card

By Marci Donley

SUPPLIES

Paper:

Sage green card and envelope,
4" x 5-1/2"

3 squares mat board,
1-1/2" x 1 3/4"

Natural rice or mulberry paper

Tools & Other Supplies:

Stamps - Small maple leaf,
skeleton leaf

Ink pad - Evergreen

2 wooden sticks, 5-1/2"
(Coffee stir sticks work great.)

Burnt orange embroidery thread

Small self-adhesive foam circles

Dimensional paper paint -
Dark green, light green, glitter

Pin back

Glue

Craft knife

Ruler

Pencil

INSTRUCTIONS

STAMP

1. Stamp the front of the card randomly, using the skeleton leaf stamp with evergreen ink. Add one or two images to the inside of the card.

2. Stamp three small maple leaves with evergreen ink on rice or mulberry paper.

ASSEMBLE

1. Position the three pieces of mat board on the front of the card. Mark a window for the middle one that is 1/4" larger on all sides than the mat board. Cut the opening. TIP: If you measure and mark from the back of the card, you can erase your pencil marks without harming the stamped images.

2. Cut the small leaves on the rice or mulberry paper to fit the mat board pieces. Glue one stamped leaf on each piece.

3. Color the edges of the mat board by pressing them on the stamp pad.

4. Cut two pieces of embroidery thread, each 8". Knot them to form a loop.

5. Using the photo as a guide, arrange the sticks and thread on the card. Glue in place.

6. Position the two outer leaf pieces over the thread loops and secure with foam dots.

7. Decorate the third stamped maple leaf with dimensional paint. (It's the pin.)

8. Glue the pin back to the stamped board piece. Let dry.

9. Pierce holes in the card for the pin back and attach the pin to the card so it shows through the cut opening. ❑

Golden Threads Mosaic

By Marci Donley

You can buy decorative paper to make this mosaic or use paper you made yourself with stamps, a multi-color pigment ink pad, dye inks, embossing powder, and a pen. Either way, it's a beautiful card.

SUPPLIES

Paper:

Textured paper card and envelope, 4-1/2" x 5"

Decorative paper with an all-over pattern

Scraps of solid color papers to coordinate with the decorative paper

Tools & Other Supplies:

Gold embroidery thread

Decorative punch

Double-sided tape

Brass plate with word (here, "ART")

2 tiny brad fasteners

Ruler

Craft knife

Glue

INSTRUCTIONS

1. Cut a piece of decorative paper to 3-3/8" x 4-5/8".

2. Cut this piece into nine smaller pieces of equal size. Keep the pieces in order so that the design looks continuous.

3. Glue the paper mosaic to the card front, leaving space for grout lines.

4. Tie gold thread around the spine of the card and wrap it in different directions around the card. Hold it in place in a few areas with tiny bits of double-sided tape.

5. Punch a solid color paper with a decorative punch. Layer it atop a scrap of gold paper. Attach to the front of the card behind the gold threads.

6. Make holes in the front of the card and attach the brass plate with tiny brad fasteners.

7. Cut a piece of decorative paper to line the inside of the card and cover the backs of the brads.

8. Decorate the envelope with a square of decorative paper and the paper scrap from the punched motif. ❏

MAKING YOUR OWN DECORATIVE PAPER

A large sheet of paper will be enough for several projects. Don't try to make a specific design - just cover the paper. Some portions will be very interesting, and some parts will look excellent!

1. Stamp a sheet of paper at random with a light color, using a stamp that creates blocks of color.
2. Stamp at random with multi-color ink, using a large background stamp.
3. Add a smaller block-type stamp in another color (perhaps a metallic).
4. Emboss the whole page with clear embossing powder.
5. Using a pen, write illegibly all over the whole sheet. (Why not tell a secret no one will be able to read?) ❏

The Road to a Friend's House

By Marnie Lyn Adams

SUPPLIES

Paper:

140 lb. soft press watercolor paper, 8-1/2" x 11" (Hot press paper may be substituted.)

Watercolor Pencils:

Black	Carmine red
Cool grey	Copenhagen
Crimson red	Dark brown

Dark green	Dark umber
French grey	Grass green
Spanish orange	Sunburst yellow
Ultramarine	

Tools & Other Supplies:

Black permanent ink pens - 03, 05, 08

Paint brushes - #2 round, 3/4" wash

10 tea bags (orange pekoe or other black tea)

1 cup water

Graphite transfer paper

Kneaded eraser

Pencil & sharpener

Ruler

Paper towels

Water container

Tracing paper

INSTRUCTIONS

PREPARE

1. Fold the watercolor paper to create a horizontal card 8-1/2" x 5-1/2".
2. Trace the pattern. Using graphite paper, transfer pattern to front of card. Use kneaded eraser to erase any mistakes.

COLOR THE DESIGN

Refer to the photo as a guide to color the design or use the colors of your choice.

BRUSH & STAIN

1. Wet colored areas, using #2 brush dampened with water. TIP: Every time you put the brush in water, blot it on a paper towel. Rinse the brush thoroughly between colors.
2. To make tea stain, heat water to boiling on stovetop or in a microwave oven. Add tea bags to water and steep for 30 minutes. Remove tea bags.
3. Using a 3/4" brush with the tea, paint entire card for an antique look. Allow to dry several hours.
4. Brush with a second coat of tea. Allow to dry overnight.

INK

1. Using the 03 pen, ink the patch outlines.
2. Using 08 pen, ink the lettering, the dots in the border, and the remainder of the design.
3. Using 05 pen, ink the small dots. ❏

PATTERN
(actual size)

Cat in the Window

By Cindy Mann Vitale

See page 62 for the pattern.

The kitty design was cut from wood to make a delightful little gift pin. If you don't wish to make the pin, you can transfer the cat pattern directly to the card.

SUPPLIES

Acrylic Craft Paint:

Barnyard red

Charcoal grey

Clay bisque

Dove gray

Italian sage

Slate blue

Sunflower

Wicker white

Artists' Acrylic Paints:

Burnt carmine

Burnt umber

Green umber

Pure black

Raw sienna

Warm white

Painting Surface:

Watercolor paper, 140-lb. cold press

White envelope to fit 5" x 7" card
 (use bubble wrap envelope if
 including the pin)

Cat wood cutout
 (Cut from 1/8" wood.)

Other Supplies:

Waterbase antiquing medium - Brown

Black permanent ink pen, size #005

Art deckle ruler

Toothbrush

Craft knife

Bar pin back, 1"

Matte sealer spray

Waterbase varnish, satin

Hot glue gun and glue sticks

Sandpaper

INSTRUCTIONS

PREPARE

1. Sand wood cutout smooth and wipe away dust.

2. Cut watercolor paper to 7" x 10-1/2". Tear one 7" edge using art deckle ruler. This will be open edge of card front. Measure and mark paper at center, then fold and crease for a 7" x 10" card with side fold.

3. Spray a light coat of matte sealer on lower left corner of envelope where design will be.

4. Transfer designs to card, wood cutout, and lower left front corner of envelope. Do not transfer any interior details.

PAINT THE DESIGN

Window:

1. Basecoat window frame with Wicker White. Shade with charcoal grey.

2. Basecoat window with dove gray. Shade some areas with slate blue and other areas with Italian sage.

Wall:

1. Basecoat with clay bisque.

2. Shade with burnt umber.

3. Paint on stripes with thinned barnyard red.

4. Basecoat red squares of checkerboard area with barnyard red. Shade them with burnt carmine.

5. Basecoat white squares of checkerboard area with warm white. Shade them with Burnt Umber.

Cat (Wood Cutout):

1. Basecoat with sunflower.

2. Shade with raw sienna.

3. When dry, transfer or freehand face design.

4. Float a light wash of barnyard red in ears.

5. Paint eyes with slate blue. Paint pupils with pure black.

6. Paint nose with burnt umber.

Heart on Cat Cutout & Envelope:

1. Basecoat above and below inset area with barnyard red. Shade these areas with burnt carmine.

2. Basecoat inset area with warm white. Shade with burnt umber.

3. Paint stripes at top and bottom of inset area with green umber.

FINISH

1. Brush wood cutout with a light, even coat of slightly diluted waterbase varnish. Let dry completely.

2. Mix equal amounts antiquing medium and water and brush on wood cutout. Use antiquing medium to stain edges and back of wood. Let dry.

3. Add linework details and outlines on wood cutout, card, and envelope with the black pen.

Continued on next page

continued from page 61

4. Spatter all surfaces with burnt umber, using the toothbrush.

5. Hot-glue pin back to backside of wood.

6. Place wood cutout in position on card design and mark on card the placement of pin's position. Cut two 1/4" vertical slits in card with craft knife on these markings. Make them close enough together to allow pin bar to side through card and fasten easily.

7. Pin card in place on card front. ❏

PATTERNS
(actual size)

Envelope design

Cat Pin

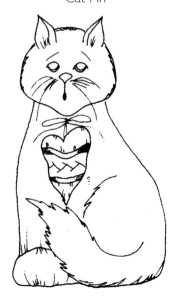

Bee-utiful Garden

PATTERNS
(actual size)

Instructions on page 64

Envelope design

Bee-utiful Garden

By Cindy Mann Vitale

This card includes a wooden pin that can be removed and worn - it adds a charming three-dimensional touch to the card. (Of course, you can paint the bee skep and daisy design on the card without making a pin.)

SUPPLIES

Painting Surfaces:

Watercolor paper, 140-lb. cold press

Envelope to fit 5" x 7" card
(Use a bubble wrap envelope to protect the pin.)

Bee skep cutout
(Cut from 1/8" wood)

Acrylic Craft Paints:

Amish blue

Barnyard red

Buttercup

Charcoal grey

Clay bisque

Huckleberry

Italian sage

Terra cotta

Artists' Acrylic Paints:

Burnt carmine

Burnt umber

Green umber

Pure black

Raw sienna

Warm white

Other Supplies:

Black permanent ink pen, size #005

Art deckle ruler

Toothbrush

Craft knife

Bar pin back, 1"

Waterbase antiquing medium - Brown

Matte sealer spray

Waterbase varnish, satin

Hot glue gun & glue sticks

Sandpaper

INSTRUCTIONS

PREPARE
1. Sand wood cutout smooth and wipe away dust.
2. Cut watercolor paper to 7" x 10-1/2". Measure and mark paper at center, then fold and crease for a 7" x 10" card with top fold.
3. Spray a light coat of matte acrylic sealer on lower left corner of envelope where design will be.
4. Transfer designs to card, wood cutout, and envelope. Do not transfer any interior details.

PAINT THE DESIGN
Stem, Leaves & Grass (Grass is also on Envelope):
1. Basecoat with Italian sage.
2. Shade with green umber.

Flower Pot:
1. Basecoat with terra cotta.
2. Shade with huckleberry.

Ladybugs:
1. Basecoat bodies with barnyard red. Shade with burnt carmine.
2. Paint dots with pure black.
3. Basecoat heads with charcoal gray. Shade with pure black.

Bees (Also on Envelope & Wood Cutout):
1. Basecoat bodies with buttercup. Shade with raw sienna.
2. Paint on stripes with pure black.
3. Paint in wings with a thin wash of warm white so that body shows through.
4. Shade wings with a very thin wash of pure black.

Background:
1. Float a thin wash of Amish blue around top of card front.
2. Float a thin wash of green umber across bottom of card front.

Bee Skep (On Wood Cutout):
1. Basecoat with clay bisque. Shade with burnt umber.
2. Paint on "ribs" with burnt umber.
3. Basecoat doorway with charcoal grey. Shade with pure black.
4. Basecoat black squares of checkerboard base with charcoal grey. Shade with pure black. Basecoat white squares with warm white and shade with burnt umber.

Daisy (On Wood Cutout):
1. Basecoat center with buttercup. Shade with raw sienna.
2. Basecoat petals with warm white. Shade with pure black.
3. Paint dots around outer edge of center with burnt umber.

FINISH
1. Brush wood cutout with a light, even coat of slightly diluted waterbase varnish. Let dry completely.
2. Mix equal amounts antiquing medium and water. Brush a light coat on wood cutout. Use antiquing medium to stain sides and back of wood. Let dry.
3. Add linework details and outlines on wood cutout, card, and envelope with the black pen.
4. Spatter all surfaces with burnt umber, using the toothbrush.
5. Hot-glue pin back to back of cutout.
6. Place cutout in position on card design and mark on card the placement of pin's position. Cut two 1/4" vertical slits in card with craft knife on these markings. Make them close enough together to allow pin bar to slide through card and fasten easily.
7. Pin card in place on card front. ❏

A Note for You

By Dolores Lennon

SUPPLIES

Paper:

Notecard with envelope, 140 lb. cold press watercolor paper

Acrylic Craft Paints:

Rose pink

Clover

Peony

Thicket

Tools & Other Supplies:

Paint brushes - #8 round, 000 liner

Paper towels

Gray transfer paper

Stylus

Waxed paper palette

Water

2 water containers (one for clean water, one for rinsing)

INSTRUCTIONS

1. Transfer designs to card and envelope.

2. Make washes of the paint colors, adding water to make a puddle of each color.

3. Using the liner brush with Clover, write "a note from [your name]."

4. Paint the flowers and leaves, using the examples on the Rose Worksheet (see the following page) as guides. ❏

Fig. 1
1. Apply a thin wash of rose pink to the entire rose in a hit or miss fashion.
2. Apply a thin wash of clover to all stems and leaves.

Fig. 2
1. Apply a thin wash of peony, scribbling the paint to indicate some rose petal sections. Apply the same color to some leaf edges.
2. Tuck a wash of thicket under the rose petals at the base of the rose. Add a thin shadow of thicket on the left side of the main stem.

3. Using a liner brush with thinned clover, add tendrils to the rose on the envelope.

a note from Elizabeth

PATTERNS
(actual size)

Envelope design

Graduation Hat & Congrats

By Marci Donley

Folded card

Envelope

SUPPLIES

Paper:

Black shiny card stock, 8-1/2" x 11"

White card stock, 8-1/2" x 11"

Black envelope, 5-3/4" square

Tools & Other Supplies:

Stamps - Congratulations, small swirl, star, diamond

Multi-color pigment ink pad

Clear embossing powder

Tassel

Glue

Gold star stickers

Craft knife

Hole punch, 1/8"

Double-sided tape

INSTRUCTIONS

CUT & FOLD

1. Cut black and white card stock to 5-1/2" x 11". Score and fold to create two 5-1/2" square cards.

2. At the fold of the white card, measure down and mark at 2-1/2" and 3". Cut 2" wide slits at marks, spanning the fold. (You will mount your pop-up tag at this section. Fig. 1.)

3. Cut a tag shape from remaining white card stock.

STAMP

1. On the tag, stamp "Congratulations" with multi-color ink. Emboss with clear powder.

2. Stamp small images randomly inside the white card in various colors from the pad. Emboss with clear powder.

3. Color the edges of the tag with the stamp pad. Let dry.

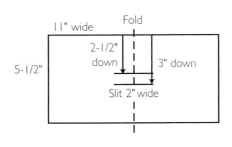

ASSEMBLE

1. Punch a small hole in the middle of the front of the black card.

2. Push the end of the tassel through the hole and secure on the back with double-sided tape. (It should look like a graduation hat.)

3. Glue the white card inside the black card, wrong sides together.

4. Secure the stamped tag to the left half of the cut slit inside the card.

5. Add a gold star sticker inside the card and another on the envelope. ❑

Feel Better

By Marci Donley

SUPPLIES

Paper:

Textured watercolor paper card and envelope, 5" x 7"

Mat board or other thick cardboard, 2-1/2" square

Tools & Other Supplies:

2" square of fabric

12" fiber, yarn, or ribbon

Heart shaped bead

Embossing tool

Removable tape

Fine point permanent black pen

Glue

Tracing paper

INSTRUCTIONS

1. Place the cardboard square on the front of the card. Hold in place with removable tape. Press around the edges with the embossing tool from the back of the card to make a recessed square on the front of the card.

2. Pull some fibers from the fabric square to fringe the edges. Glue the fabric at the center of the recessed square.

3. Arrange the fiber, yarn, or ribbon and the heart bead at the center of the square and secure with glue.

4. Practice writing your message in small lower case letters with the black pen on a sheet of tracing paper. Hold the tracing paper over the card to determine the placement. Write the greeting on the card. ❏

The pressed leaves in the rice paper card make an interesting background for this painted leaves design.

Thank You

By Dolores Lennon

PATTERN
Enlarge @155% for actual size.

SUPPLIES

Paper:
Rice paper notecard with envelope

Acrylic Craft Paint:
Holiday red Thicket Yellow ochre

Tools & Other Supplies:
Black permanent ink pen, 005
Paint brush - #8 round
Paper towels • Transfer paper & stylus
Water • Waxed paper palette
2 water containers (one for clean water, one for rinsing)

INSTRUCTIONS

PREPARE
1. Trace the design and transfer to the notecard. Don't press too hard while transferring.
2. Ink the design lines.
3. Make a wash of each color on the palette pad.

PAINT THE DESIGN
Use the examples on the Leaves Worksheet as guides.
1. Dampen each leaf with water, using the round brush. (Fig. 1)
2. Pick up some yellow ochre and dab on leaves. (Fig. 1)
3. Apply a wash of thicket to the center leaf. Let dry. (Fig. 1)
4. Dampen the leaves with clean water. (Fig. 2)
5. Apply a holiday red wash to each leaf. (Fig. 2)
6. Add thinned thicket or holiday red for vein lines. (Fig. 2) ❏

Leaves Worksheet

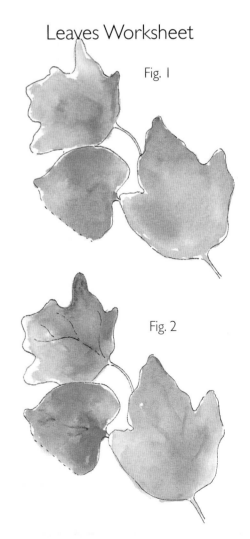

Fig. 1

Fig. 2

Better Soon

Marci Donley

This card is a decoupaged collage, but to make it you don't need to use decoupage papers - you can find a wealth of images in catalogs, magazines, and most junk mail. I like to keep a scrap box of leftovers from other projects and small pieces of gift wrap. When I see an image I like, I cut it out and add it to the box.

SUPPLIES

Paper:

Card and envelope, 5" x 7"

Decoupage papers or gift wrap - various prints, plus paper with letters

Tools & Other Supplies:

Decoupage medium

Beads

Needle and gold thread

Scissors

INSTRUCTIONS

1. Cut or tear interesting pieces or patterns from decoupage papers or gift wrap.

2. Arrange the designs on the card. Glue in place with decoupage finish. Use decoupage finish to glue some small beads, too.

3. Cut out letters for your message. Glue in place. You can put part of the message inside the card.

4. Enhance your collage with strung beads. Sew them to the card with gold thread.

5. Cut a piece of paper to cover the back of the card front to hide your threads and knots. Glue in place.

6. Use paper and letters to decorate the envelope. ❑

Thank You - I Can't Say It Enough

By Marci Donley

I made a Thank You card, but you could use this technique for other greetings.
You also can make several "one of a kind" cards in one sitting.

SUPPLIES

Paper:

Green, yellow, and purple paper and/or card stock

Black photo frame card and envelope, 5" x 7"

Non-reproducing blue grid paper

Option: White paper

Tools & Other Supplies:

Assorted pens with black ink

Photocopier *or* scanner and computer printer

Small black grommets and setting tools

Glue

INSTRUCTIONS

1. Write the words "Thank You" many different ways with different pens on non-reproducing blue grid paper, using the patterns provided or writing freehand. Cover an area that is larger than the front of the card so you can use different portions of it at different times. *Option:* If you plan to use a scanner, don't write directly on the grid paper - the blue lines will reproduce. Instead, put the grid paper behind a piece of white paper; you can use the lines but they won't show.

   • Try to create a nice pattern. Remember you will be cutting, pasting, shrinking, and enlarging your words so don't fret if it doesn't seem perfect to you.

   • If you make a mistake or want to make a change you can use correction fluid or cut and paste - you will not be using this sheet directly on the card.

2. Copy the sheet over and over in different sizes on different colors of paper, using a photocopier. *Option:* Scan and print.

3. Cut and place sizes and shapes together to create a pleasing design. Glue in place.

4. Highlight the message with a large "Thank You" cutout with a lined border. Glue, then insert a grommet in each corner to accent.

5. Glue a strip of colored paper with your message along the left side of the envelope. ❏

PATTERN

Enlarge @145% for actual size.

Option: photocopy this onto your colored paper.

Cards for Spring & Summer Holidays

This section includes cards for holidays in the spring and summer seasons -
Valentine's Day, Easter, Mother's Day, and Father's Day.

Mother's Day Petal Card

By Marci Donley

Pounded flowers color a watercolor paper insert inside a folded petaled flower card. Embossed decorative paper makes a beautiful petaled flower.

Instructions begin on page 78.

Mother's Day Petal Card
Pictured on page 77

SUPPLIES

Paper:

Decorative paper 12" square

Watercolor paper, 5" x 6"

Envelope, 6-1/2" square

Vellum

Other Supplies:

Freshly picked flowers

Wax paper

Hammer

20" ribbon, 1/4" wide

Stamp - Mom

Pigment ink

Embossing powder - Verdigris

Hole punch, 1/8"

Decorative edge scissors

INSTRUCTIONS

CUT

1. Cut the decorative paper, using the pattern provided. Remember to cut on the solid lines and fold on the dotted lines.

2. Make a vellum template for the card inside the folded flower.

POUND FLOWERS

As with any new technique, practice on some scrap paper until you get the right feel.

1. Trim the stems and any exceptionally thick parts off the flowers.

2. Place a flower face down on the watercolor paper. Cover with wax paper. Using a hammer, pound the flower through the wax paper - you will see the flower colors transfer to the paper. Repeat with other flowers.

3. When you have a nice arrangement, use the template to cut the watercolor paper to fit inside the folded petal card.

ASSEMBLE

1. Cut a smaller shape of vellum using decorative scissors. Write a message on it. Punch holes and attach it to the pounded flower design with a ribbon.

2. Fold the petals of the flower with the six-sided card inside.

3. Make a layered tag for the outside of the flower petal card, using papers from the project. Stamp MOM and emboss.

4. If you're not mailing the card, add a layered, embossed label and a bow to the envelope. ❑

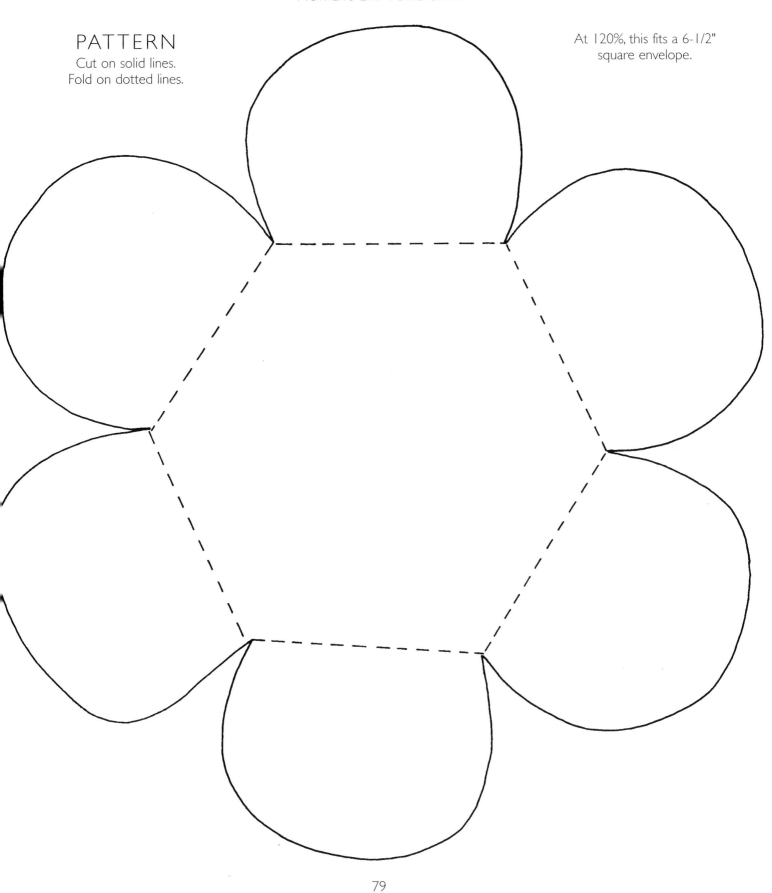

PATTERN
Cut on solid lines.
Fold on dotted lines.

At 120%, this fits a 6-1/2"
square envelope.

Lacy Valentine

By Marci Donley

SUPPLIES

Paper:

Red card stock, 5-1/2" x 8-1/2"

White envelope, 6-1/8" x 5"

White, small piece

Gold, small piece

Vellum, small piece

Other Supplies:

Background stamp - Rose vine

Greeting stamp

Stamp ink pads - Cinnamon

Embossing powder - white

Heat tool

29" white organdy ribbon, 1" wide

Decorative edge scissors

Mizuhiki (Japanese wrapped decorative cord)

Red ribbon rose

Glue

Self-adhesive foam circles

Optional: Small piece of red organdy ribbon (for envelope)

INSTRUCTIONS

FOLD & STAMP

1. Measure 2-1/8" in from the short ends of the red card stock. Score and fold ends to meet in the middle.

2. Stamp all over the red paper with the cinnamon ink, using the rose background stamp. You will have a faint pattern in a color slightly darker than the paper. Do not

non ink.

ler.

of white

the

old

ing

ly.

d as

s on

llest

heart.

7. *Option:* Stamp some vellum with the rose background stamp to make a liner for your envelope. Decorate the envelope with a heart cutout and a small piece of ribbon. ❏

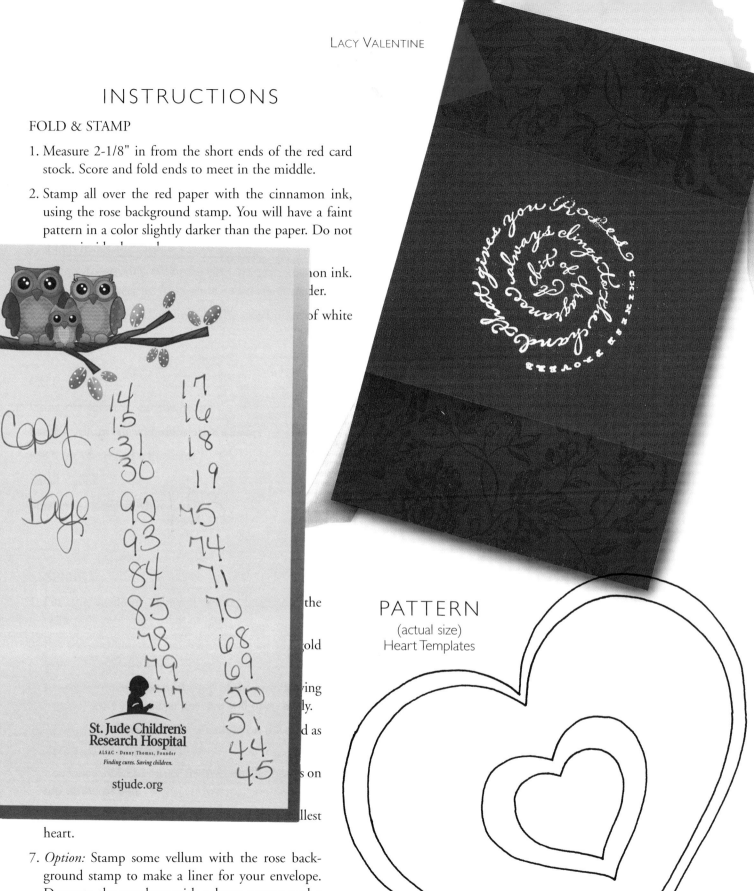

PATTERN
(actual size)
Heart Templates

Copper Valentine

By Marci Donley

Thin copper sheeting is used to decorate the front and inside of this card. I like how the heart inside the card swings on the grommet that's used to attach it.

SUPPLIES

Paper:

4" x 5" ochre colored card and envelope

Metallic gold paper

Tools & Other Supplies:

40 gauge copper sheeting

Brass stencil with hearts

Stylus (A ballpoint pen that has run out of ink makes a great stylus.)

Grommets and setting tools

Gold thread

Ruler

Small copper washer

Glue

Gold paint pen

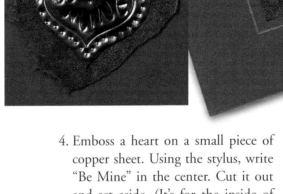

Inside of card

INSTRUCTIONS

EMBOSS THE COPPER

1. Cut a piece of copper sheeting 3-3/4" x 4-3/4".
2. Place the stencil on the copper and trace the edges of the design with the stylus tool. Fill in spaces with your own designs, using the stylus tool like you would a pencil.
3. Use a ruler and the stylus to create a border on the copper sheet.
4. Emboss a heart on a small piece of copper sheet. Using the stylus, write "Be Mine" in the center. Cut it out and set aside. (It's for the inside of the card.)
5. Use a non-heat conducting clamp to hold the pieces of copper over a flame. (The copper changes color when it is heated.) Don't touch it until you are sure it is cooled. TIP: Practice with an extra piece of copper.

ASSEMBLE

1. Use grommets (one in each corner) to attach the copper rectangle to the front of the card.
2. Stitch the gold thread in and out of the grommets to add a finished and textured look to the front of the card. Finish off the ends in a bow at the top center. Glue the copper washer at the center of the bow.
3. Tear a small piece of metallic gold paper. Use one grommet to attach the heart inside the card with the paper behind the heart.

DECORATE ENVELOPE

1. Cut out and glue a metallic paper "label" on the front of the envelope.
2. Outline the label with a gold paint pen. ❏

Happy Father's Day

By Marci Donley

Color photocopy a favorite photo and transfer to watercolor paper to get a grainy look. Or use a black and white photo and add a bit of soft color here and there with colored pencils.

INSTRUCTIONS

1. Using the color copy, transfer the photo to the watercolor paper, following the instructions for "Photo Transfers" in the Special Techniques section.

2. Tear the edges of the transferred photo, using a decorative edge ruler.

3. Fold the black card stock. Place the mulberry paper on the front. Place the transferred photo over the mulberry paper. Glue in place.

4. Stamp the message on a scrap of black card. Emboss the message with verdigris powder. Cut the shape to fit the card.

5. Stamp fish on watercolor paper. Color with pencils.

6. Tie the fish on pieces of thread. Loop the thread pieces over the stamped message. Glue to card, letting the fish dangle.

7. Stamp a fish and emboss "DAD" on the envelope. ❏

SUPPLIES

Paper:

Color copy of photograph

White soft watercolor paper, 5" x 7"

Black card stock,
    5-1/2" x 8-1/2" plus scraps

Mulberry paper (a color that enhances the photo), 5" x 4"

White envelope, 5-3/4" x 4-3/8"

Other Supplies:

Acetone

Cotton Ball

Burnisher

Stamps - Fish, alphabet

Colored pencils

Ink Pad - Black waterproof

Pigment or embossing ink

Embossing powder - Verdigris

12" heavy thread or light string

Decorative edge ruler

Glue

Scissors

Easter Basket

By Marci Donley

SUPPLIES

Paper:

Sage heavy paper, 3-1/2" x 7" plus more to make the envelope

Lavender heavy paper, 3-1/2" x 7"

Yellow card stock, 3-1/2" x 4-1/2"

Pink card stock, 3-1/2" x 4-1/2"

Tools & Other Supplies:

Stamp - 3" egg

Ink pads - Heliotrope, lime

1 sq. ft. purple netting

Decorative edge scissors

Scissors

Ribbons - Lavender satin, iridescent, 1/4" wide

Flat-backed charm

Glue

PATTERNS
(actual size)

Cut on solid lines.
Fold on dotted lines.

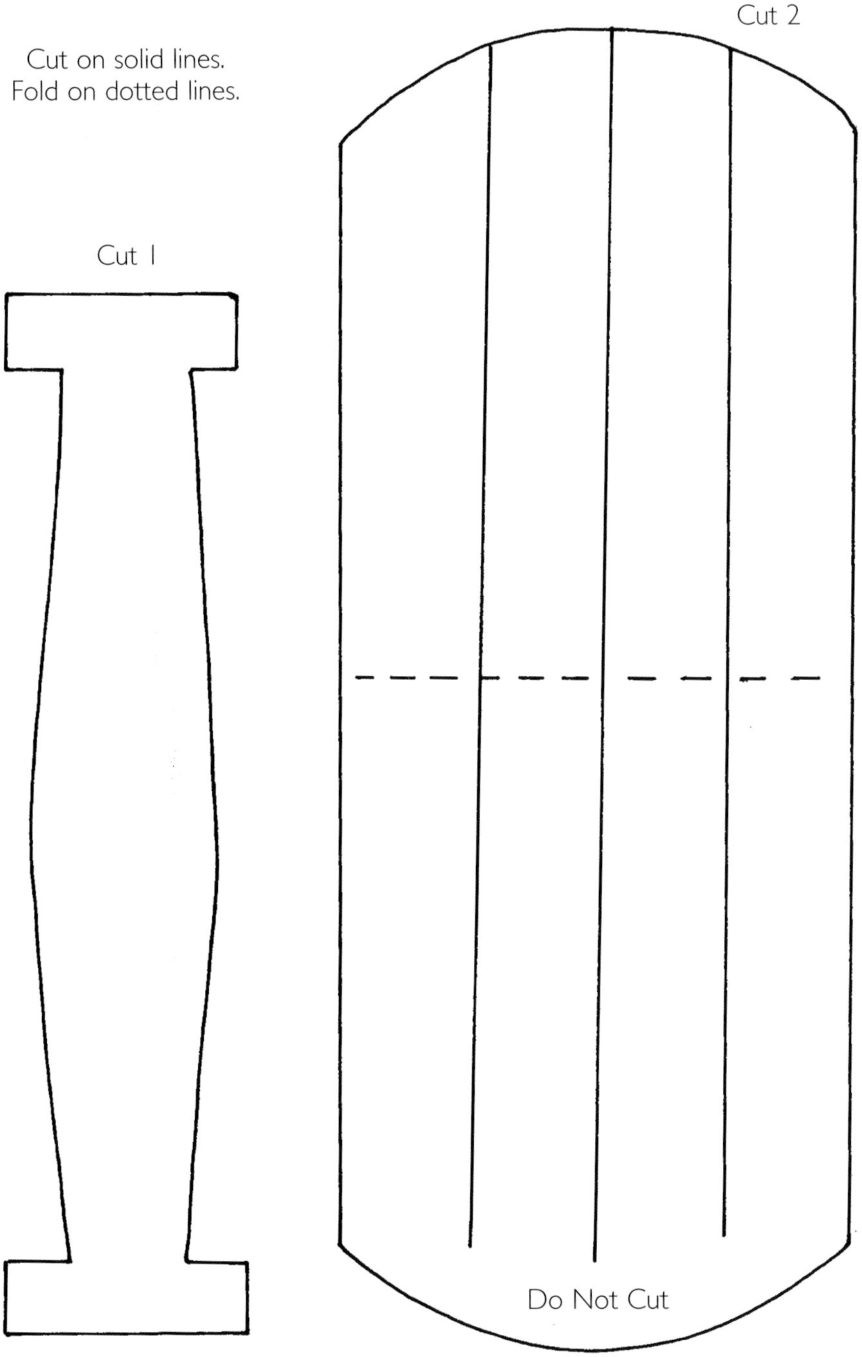

Cut 1

Cut 2

Do Not Cut

INSTRUCTIONS

MAKE THE BASKET

1. Using the patterns provided, cut one basket in each color and one handle from lavender. Use decorative edge scissors to cut the outer edges and the handle. Use straight scissors for the interior cuts on the basket and the ends of the handle.

2. Fold the basket pieces as indicated. Leave one end of each piece uncut; be sure the other end is cut all the way through.

3. Weave the two pieces together, working until you reach the fold. Then fold and complete the weaving.

4. Cut slits for the handle and insert. Glue in place.

5. Glue the open and unattached woven ends in place.

6. Decorate the basket with ribbons and charm.

FINISH

1. On pink card stock, stamp two eggs with heliotrope ink right next to each other so that the pointed ends touch one another. Cut out, leaving them attached. Fold at the attachment to make an egg-shaped card.

2. Stamp two eggs on yellow card stock with lime ink. Cut out and fold the same way.

3. Gather up the netting at the center and slip it in the basket. Trim as necessary.

4. Write messages on the egg cards and slip them in the basket.

5. Stamp the egg randomly on sage paper with lime ink. Cut with decorative edge scissors and use to line envelope. ❑

Happily Ever After

Use a special card to mark a special occasion - to acknowledge an important event in someone else's life or your own. In this section you'll find cards for weddings, anniversaries, and birth announcements.

Bride's Card

Instructions begin on page 88.

Bride's Card

By Marnie Lyn Adams

Pictured on page 87

SUPPLIES

Paper:

140 lb. soft press watercolor paper, 8-1/2" x 11" (Hot press paper may be substituted.)

Watercolor Pencils:

Blush pink

Carmine red

Copenhagen

Cream

Crimson red

Dark brown

Dark green

Grass green

Light peach

Non-repro blue

Tools & Other Supplies:

Black permanent ink pen - 03

Paint brushes - #2 round, #6 round

Graphite transfer paper

Kneaded eraser

Pencil & sharpener

Ruler

Paper towels

Water container

Tracing paper

INSTRUCTIONS

PREPARE & INK

1. Fold the watercolor paper to create a vertical card 5-1/2" x 8-1/2".

2. Trace pattern. Using graphite paper, transfer pattern to front of card. Use kneaded eraser to erase any mistakes.

3. Using the pen, ink the entire design.

COLOR

Use the project photo as a guide.

1. With cream, color the veil, the lace on the bouquet, and the train.

2. With light peach, color the face and the neck.

3. With blush pink, color the cheeks and one-third of the roses.

4. With carmine red, color another one-third of the roses.

5. With crimson red, color the lips and the remaining one-third of the roses.

6. With grass green, color half the leaves.

7. With dark green, color the other half of the leaves.

8. With non-repro blue, color the background.

9. With copenhagen, color the bows and the ribbon.

10. With dark brown, color the hair and the eyebrows.

BRUSH

Wet the colored areas, using a brush dampened with water. Use #6 brush for the background and #2 brush for remainder of the design. Rinse thoroughly between colors. Allow to dry overnight. TIP: Every time you rinse the brush in water, blot it on a paper towel. ❏

PATTERN

(actual size)

Layered Wedding Cake

By Marci Donley

SUPPLIES

Paper:

Apricot card, 5" x 7",
   and matching envelope

White glossy card stock,
   6" x 5" plus a small scrap

Contrasting paper,
   4-1/4" x 6-1/4" plus a small scrap

Mulberry or rice paper,
   3-1/2" x 5-1/2"

Tools & Other Supplies:

Brass stencil - Wedding cake

Embossing tool - stylus

18" sheer ribbon,
   7/8" wide

Decorative corner punch

Round hole punches,
   1" and 1-1/4"

Self-adhesive foam circles,
   large and small

2 white ribbon roses

Glue

INSTRUCTIONS

1. Use the decorative corner punch to trim the corners of the contrasting paper.

2. Glue the contrasting paper, then the mulberry or rice paper to the front of the card.

3. Fold the glossy card stock in half to make a card 2-1/2" x 3".

4. Emboss a wedding cake on the front of the glossy card.

5. Loop the ribbon on card front and use foam dots to hold it in place.

6. Place foam dots on the back of the glossy card and position it on top.

(I used one in each corner and a couple in the center so I didn't get a saggy cake.)

7. Glue two flowers above and below the card.

8. Emboss a bride and groom on a scrap of glossy paper and punch with the 1" punch.

9. Punch a piece of the contrast paper with the 1-1/4" punch.

10. Layer the circles with a foam dot in between. Use as a seal for the envelope. ❏

Wedding Cake Stencil

90

Baby Bib Card

By Marci Donley

SUPPLIES

Paper:

Art paper in two shades of blue

Tools & Other Supplies:

Hole punch, 1/8"

12" iridescent ribbon, 1/4" wide

12" blue satin ribbon, 1/8" wide

Stencils - Alphabet, flowers

Tiny sponge applicators

Stamp ink pads - Blue, lavender

Dimensional paper paints -
 Blue, white, black, pink

Black pen

Scissors

Craft knife

INSTRUCTIONS

CUT & STENCIL

1. Use the patterns provided to cut the bib, pocket, bear, and bottle. Use the photo as a guide for colors.

2. Stencil B-A-B-Y on the pocket of the bib. Stencil flowers randomly on the bib. (I blended the blue and lavender inks for stenciling and used sponge applicators.)

3. Cut out an envelope from art paper.

ASSEMBLE

1. Glue the pocket to the bib.

2. Using the dimensional paper paint, paint stitch marks around the edges of the bib and the envelope flaps. Add painted accents to the bottle and bear. Let dry.

3. Use the black pen to write a greeting on the bottle and bear.

4. Punch holes in the bib. Make a tie with the blue ribbon. Use the iridescent ribbon to attach the bottle and the bear to the bib.

5. Glue envelope. ❏

See page 94 for patterns.

Baby Bib Card
PATTERNS
(actual size)

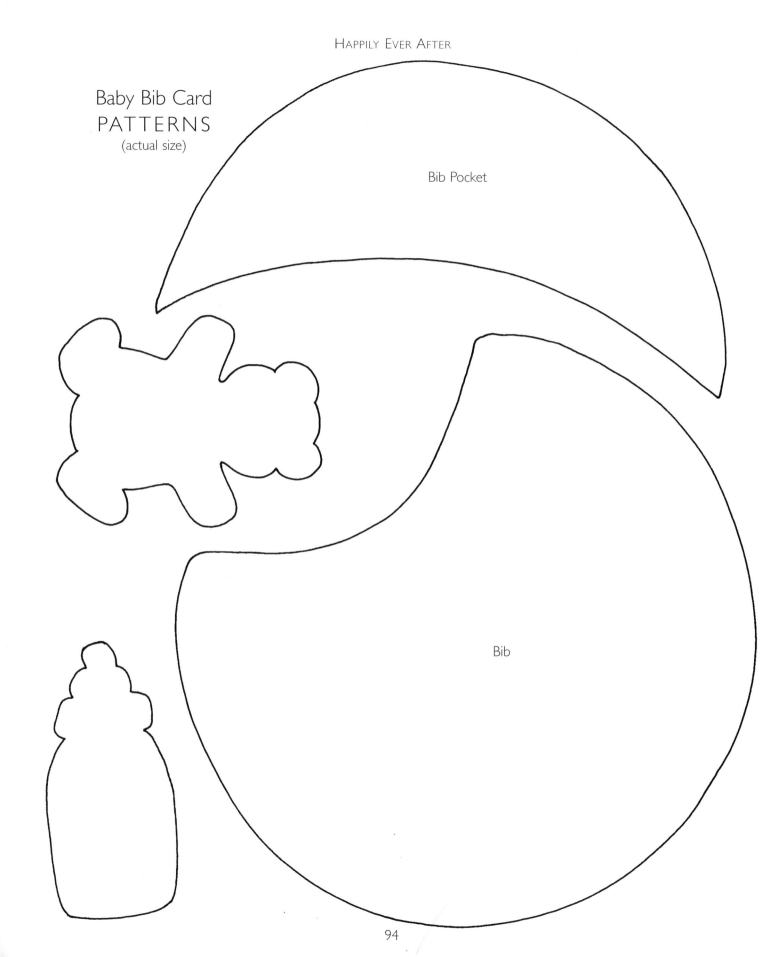

Bib Pocket

Bib

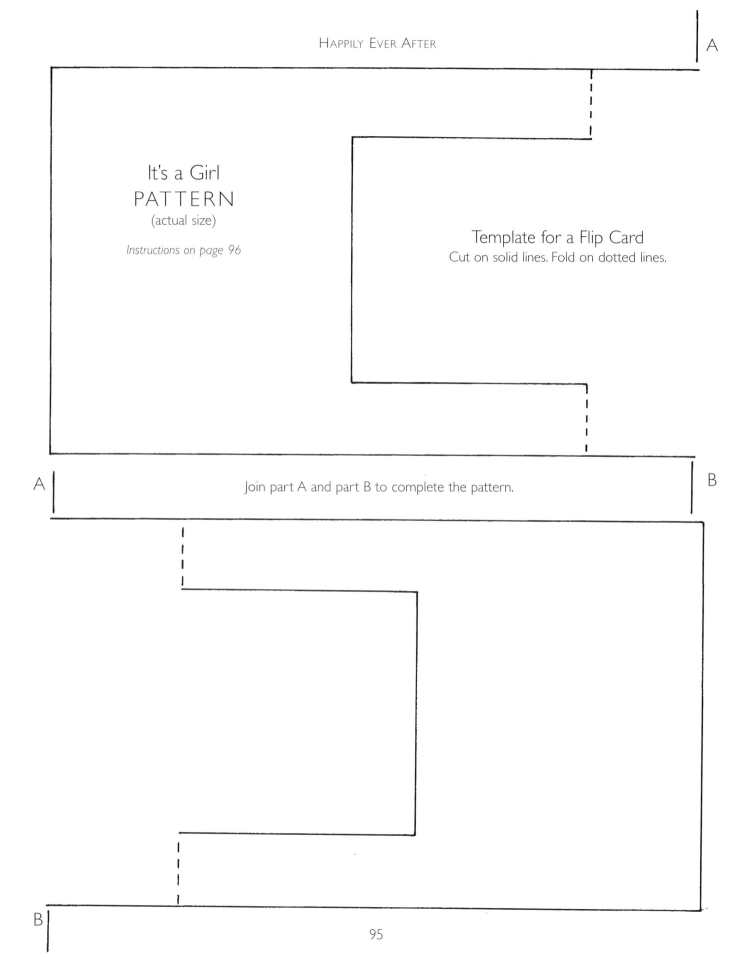

A

It's a Girl
PATTERN
(actual size)

Instructions on page 96

Template for a Flip Card
Cut on solid lines. Fold on dotted lines.

B

A

Join part A and part B to complete the pattern.

B

B

It's a Girl Birth Announcement

By Marci Donley

SUPPLIES

Paper:

Pink tinted watercolor paper, 14" x 4"

Pink tinted watercolor paper envelope, 9-1/2" x 4"

Deep pink paper, 2-3/8" x 4-3/4"

Tools & Other Supplies:

Stamps - Baby motifs background, swirl alphabet

Stamp ink pads - Cinnamon, seashell

Baby photo

Pressed pink flowers

Craft knife

Glue

Optional: Transparent sticker

INSTRUCTIONS

1. Using the patterns provided, make a template. Cut out the card. Score and fold on the dotted lines.

2. Stamp all over the front of the card, using the background stamp with the seashell ink.

3. Stamp "It's a Girl" on the front in cinnamon ink and "Name:," "Born:," "Weight:," and "Length:" (or any message you prefer) on the back of the card.

4. Trim the photo 1/4" smaller than part of the card that shows when the card is closed.

5. Adhere the deep pink paper rectangle to the area of the card where the photo will be. Adhere the photo to the paper.

6. Glue pressed flowers to the front of the card and to one corner of the envelope. *Option:* If you're mailing the envelope, place a transparent sticker over the flowers. ❏

Ark & Animals

By Marnie Lyn Adams

SUPPLIES

Paper:

140 lb. cold press watercolor paper, 8-1/2" x 11"

Watercolor Pencils:

Black

Crimson red

Grass green

Spanish orange

Ultramarine

Colored Pencils:

Black

Crimson red

Grass green

Spanish orange

Ultramarine

Tools & Other Supplies:

Black permanent ink pens - 03, 05, 08

Paint brushes - #2 round, #6 round

Graphite transfer paper

Kneaded eraser

Pencil & sharpener

Ruler

Paper towels

Water container

Tracing paper

PATTERN
Inside Lettering

You two make a Beautiful couple !

INSTRUCTIONS

PREPARE

1. Fold the watercolor paper to create a vertical card 5-1/2" x 8-1/2".

2. Trace pattern. Using graphite paper, transfer pattern to front of card. Use kneaded eraser to erase any mistakes.

COLOR WITH WATERCOLOR PENCILS

Use the project photo as a guide.

1. With the spanish orange watercolor pencil, color the blocks behind "ark and animals", "E", "j", "noah", "u", and "x" (but leave the lettering white).

2. With the crimson red watercolor pencil, color the blocks behind "B", "f", "i", "m", "P", "Two by 2", "y", and the four corner blocks (but leave the lettering white).

3. With the ultramarine watercolor pencil, color the blocks behind "c","G", "k", "q", "rain", "w", "z", and the top and bottom border blocks (but leave the lettering white).

4. With the grass green watercolor pencil, color the blocks behind "dove", "H", "L", "O", "S", "v", and the two side border blocks (but leave the lettering white).

5. With the black watercolor pencil, color the borders around the blocks.

BRUSH

Wet the colored areas, using a brush dampened with water. Use the #6 brush for larger areas and the #2 brush for smaller areas around lettering. Allow to dry overnight. TIP: Every time the brush is put in water, blot it on a paper towel. Rinse the brush thoroughly between colors.

INK

1. With 03 pen, ink the block outlines.

2. Using 05 pen, ink the lettering.

COLOR WITH COLORED PENCILS

Use the photo as a guide.

1. With the spanish orange colored pencil, shade lettering and add dotted line to blocks behind "ark and animals", "E", "j", "noah", "u", and "X".

2. With the crimson red colored pencil, shade lettering and add corner lines to blocks behind "B", "f", "i", "m", "P", "Two by 2", and "y". Add spirals to the corner blocks.

3. With the ultramarine colored pencil, shade lettering and add slash lines to blocks behind "c", "G", "k", "q", "rain", "w", and "z". Add waves to the top and bottom border blocks.

4. With the grass green colored pencil, shade the lettering and add corner Xs to blocks behind "dove", "H", "L", "O", "S", and "v". Add dash lines to the side border blocks.

ADD MESSAGE

1. Using graphite paper, transfer the message pattern to the inside of the card. Use kneaded eraser to erase any mistakes.

2. Using an 08 pen, ink the message. ❑

PATTERN

(actual size)

Happy Anniversary

By Marci Donley

SUPPLIES

Paper:

Purchased card and envelope, 5" x 7"

Vellum, 4" x 6"

Tools & Other Supplies:

1" square dye ink stamping pads in 4 colors

Alphabet letter stamps to spell L-O-V-E

Gold pigment ink

Gold embossing powder

Foil and foil glue

Fine or micro point black pen

Craft knife

Pencil

Ruler

White eraser

INSTRUCTIONS

1. Mark an area on the front of the card that will accommodate four 1" stamped squares and a border. Cut out with craft knife.

2. Apply a foil border around the edges of the cutout, following the manufacturer's instructions.

3. With the card closed, lightly draw a pencil mark around the area cutout area inside the card.

4. Stamp four squares inside of the card. Let dry.

5. Stamp the letters (L-O-V-E) with gold ink. Emboss with gold powder.

6. Use a ruler and black pen to draw lines around the stamped blocks.

7. Glue the vellum to the inside of the front of the card.

8. Practice writing "Happy Anniversary." Pencil or transfer to the front of the card. Take a deep breath to relax and write in black ink. Let dry.

9. Clean up all your pencil marks with a white eraser.

10. Use the stamping squares and the black pen to create a coordinating design on the envelope. ❏

You're Invited

The start of a special party is a special party invitation. This section includes
four invitations for a variety of parties.

Garden Party Invitation
Instructions on page 103

Garden Party Invitation

By Dolores Lennon

SUPPLIES

Paper:
140 lb. cold press watercolor paper cut to 4" x 6"

Acrylic Craft Paints:
Hydrangea
Light peony
Dark hydrangea
Clover
Peony

Tools & Other Supplies:
Black permanent ink pen, 005
Paint brush - #8 round
Paper towels
Gray transfer paper & stylus
Tracing paper
Waxed paper palette
2 water containers (one for clean water, one for rinsing)

INSTRUCTIONS

PREPARE

1. Trace and transfer the design to the postcard.

2. Ink the design.

3. Make washes of all paint colors on the waxed palette.

PAINT THE DESIGN

Use the examples on the Garden Gloves Worksheet as guides.

1. Apply a wash of hydrangea to top edges of gloves and the left sides of fingers. (Fig. 1)

2. Apply a wash of light peony to roses. (Fig. 1)

3. Apply a wash of clover to the leaves. (Fig. 1)

4. Apply a wash of dark hydrangea to the small flowers on the seam and to create a shadow to the left of the rose cluster. (Fig. 2)

5. Apply a circular swiggle of peony to each rose. (Fig. 2)

6. Dampen the area all around the design with clean water. Apply scant washes of peony, clover, and dark hydrangea. (Fig. 3) ❏

See page 104 for pattern.

Fig. 1

Garden Gloves Worksheet

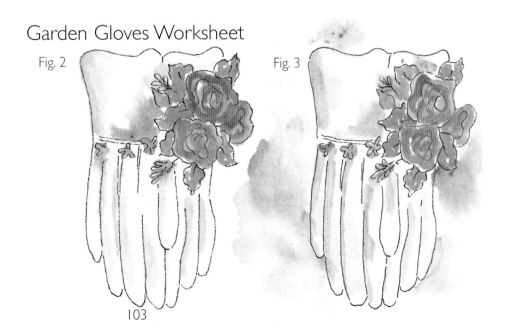

Fig. 2

Fig. 3

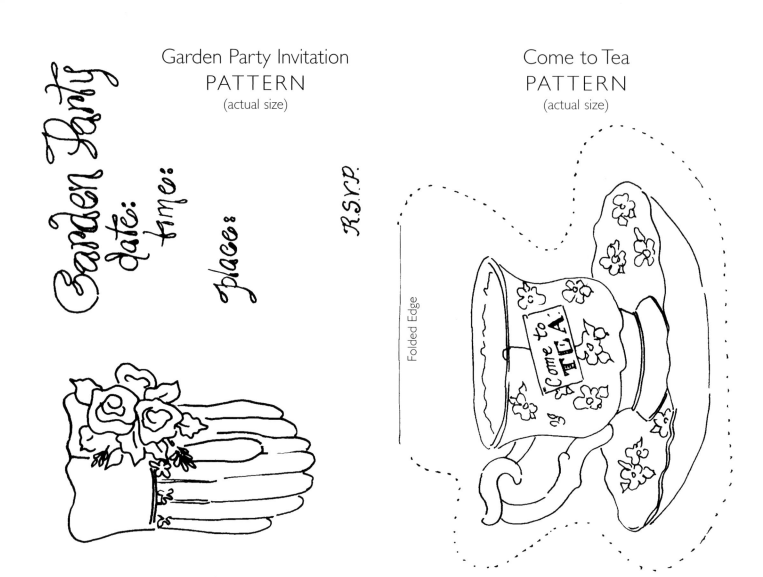

Garden Party
date: time:
place:
R.S.V.P.

Garden Party Invitation
PATTERN
(actual size)

Come to Tea
PATTERN
(actual size)

Folded Edge

Come to TEA

Teacup Worksheet

Fig. 1

Fig. 2

Come to TEA

Come to TEA

Come to Tea

By Dolores Lennon

SUPPLIES

Paper:

140 lb. cold press watercolor notecard with envelope, 3-1/2" x 5"

Acrylic Craft Paints:

Autumn leaves

Dark hydrangea

Hydrangea

Nutmeg

Peony

Pure gold (metallic)

Thicket

Tools & Other Supplies:

Black permanent ink pen - 005

Paint brushes - #8 round, liner

Paper towels

Scissors

Gray transfer paper & stylus

Tracing paper & pencil

Waxed paper palette

2 water containers (one for clean water, one for rinsing)

INSTRUCTIONS

PREPARE

1. Following the dots on the pattern, cut out the card, echoing the shape of the teacup and saucer.
2. Ink the design.
3. Make washes of each color on your palette.

PAINT THE DESIGN

Use the examples on the Teacup Worksheet as guides.

1. Dampen the edges of the teacup and saucer with clean water. Apply a Hydrangea wash. (Fig. 1)
2. Add touches of dark hydrangea to shadow areas. (Fig. 1)
3. Apply a wash of nutmeg to inside of teacup. (This is the tea.) (Fig. 1)
4. Add a very thin wash of nutmeg to the teabag label. (Fig. 1)
5. Apply a wash of peony to the teacup and saucer. (Fig. 2)
6. Paint the little flowers with dabs of thinned peony, applying the color with the tip of the brush. (Fig. 2) Don't forget to add a flower to the envelope.
7. Touch down a bit of thinned thicket for the leaf shapes. (Fig. 2)
8. Using a liner brush, color the centers of the flowers with dots of autumn leaves.
9. Add a wash of peony to the tea in the cup.
10. Edge the cup and saucer with thinned pure gold metallic, using the liner brush. ❏

You're Invited

By Dolores Lennon

SUPPLIES

Paper:

140 lb. cold press watercolor paper cut to 4" x 6"

Acrylic Craft Paints:

Cardinal red

Clover

Peony

Purple

Sunflower

Tools & Other Supplies:

Black permanent ink pen - #005

Paint brushes - #8 round, #000

Paper towels

Gray transfer paper & stylus

Tracing paper & pencil

Waxed paper palette

2 water containers (one for clean water, one for rinsing)

INSTRUCTIONS

PREPARE

1. Trace and transfer the design.

2. Ink the design.

3. Make washes of each color.

PAINT THE DESIGN

Use the examples on the Flowers & Bee Worksheet as guides.

1. Apply a wash of purple to top wild rose and lower right flower. (Fig. 1)

2. Apply a wash of peony to the center chrysanthemum and the lower left wildflower. (Fig. 1)

3. Fill flower centers and bee's body with washes of sunflower. (Fig. 1)

PATTERN
(actual size)

4. Apply a clover wash to stems and leaves. (Fig. 1)

5. Add a wash of cardinal red to top wild rose. (Fig. 2)

6. Add a purple wash to the center chrysanthemum. (Fig. 2)
   ❑

Flowers & Bee Worksheet

Fig. 1

Fig. 2

Please Come to Our Party

By Marci Donley

This invitation has a pocket made from paper you decorate yourself in the style of an altered book. Don't worry how the writing looks - you are simply adding pattern and texture to the paper. It doesn't need to be legible or make sense, it's a good way to work out some tension! I wrote "Please Come to Our Party" on one tag, "Date:," "Time:," "Place:," and "RSVP" on a second tag, and "Your Admission Ticket" on the back of the second tag. You can add the information with a light colored gel pen.

SUPPLIES

Paper:

Corrugated paper, 7" square

Sage green paper, 6" square

Green vellum, 6" square

Black card stock, 11" square (for envelope)

2 black tags, each 3" x 6"

Tools & Other Supplies:

Black fine-tip permanent pen

Stamp ink pads - Gold, silver, green chalk, cocoa

Erasable pen *or* embossing pen

Gold embossing powder

Assorted ribbons and yarns

Glue

Scissors or craft knife

INSTRUCTIONS

DECORATE PAPERS

1. Cut vellum diagonally to make a triangle shape.

2. Write all over the green paper and the vellum with the black pen. Let dry.

3. Apply inks directly to the paper, smearing the color here and there. Let dry.

EMBOSS & GLUE

1. Use the erasable pen (or any embossing pen) and write your words on the tag. Emboss with the gold powder. TIP: Work one side at a time, and work quickly.

2. Glue the green decorated paper to the corrugated square. Glue the vellum triangle on top of the decorative paper, leaving the long edge open to form a pocket.

MAKE ENVELOPE

1. Score a 7-1/4" square in the center of the 11" square card for the envelope. Fold in the corners and cut excess from areas that overlap for a flatter fold.

2. Pierce two holes in the square and thread 40" of ribbon or yarn through the holes for ties.

ASSEMBLE

1. Tie the two tags together with some ribbons and yarns.

2. Put the tags in the pocket of the card.

3. Place the card in the envelope, fold up the flaps, and tie it shut. ❏

Winter
Holiday Cards

Winter holidays are often the time of year when we make the effort to keep in touch with faraway friends. Handmade holiday cards are a lovely way to send personal greetings of the season and messages for the new year.

Mr. Snowman

By Cindy Mann Vitale

Instructions begin on page 112.

Mr. Snowman

Pictured on page 111

SUPPLIES

Painting Surfaces:

Watercolor paper, 140 lb. cold press

White card with navy edge, 5" x 6-7/8"

White envelope to fit 5" x 7" card

Acrylic Craft Paints:

Acorn brown

Amish blue

Autumn leaves

Barnyard red

Buttercup

Clay bisque

Country twill

Huckleberry

Indigo

Italian sage

Maple syrup

Slate blue

Wicker white

Artists' Acrylic Paints:

Burnt carmine

Burnt umber

Green umber

Pure black

Raw sienna

Warm white

Other Supplies:

Black permanent ink pen, size 005

Toothbrush

Double stick mounting tape

Linen string

Thick white craft glue

Matte sealer spray

Here the snowman is painted on watercolor paper, cut out, and made into a tree ornament. The card is painted only with the snow and tree background, and the paper ornament is attached to the card. It's a card and a gift - a lovely ornament to hang on the holiday tree.

INSTRUCTIONS

PREPARE

1. Transfer ornament design (snowman) to a 4" x 6-1/2" piece of watercolor paper.

2. Lightly spray an even coat of matte acrylic sealer on card and lower left corner of envelope where design will be.

3. Transfer designs to card and envelope. Do not transfer any interior details.

PAINT THE DESIGN

Snowman Ornament:

1. Basecoat with warm white. Shade with slate blue.

2. Transfer nose and pipe. *Option:* Paint freehand.

3. Basecoat nose with autumn leaves. Shade with huckleberry.

4. Basecoat pipe with buttercup. Shade with raw sienna.

5. Basecoat hat with country twill. Shade with burnt umber. When dry, transfer or freehand the hole. Paint the hole in hat with pure black.

6. Basecoat bird with barnyard red. Shade with burnt carmine. Paint beak with buttercup.

7. Basecoat scarf with clay bisque. Shade with burnt umber. Basecoat inner stripes with Amish blue and shade with indigo. Basecoat edge trim areas with barnyard red and shade with burnt carmine.

8. Basecoat sweater with Italian sage. Shade with green umber. Basecoat cuffs with barnyard red and shade with burnt carmine. Basecoat design area with warm white and shade with burnt umber. Transfer or freehand pine branch (not needles). Paint branch with burnt umber. Paint needles with green umber. Make dots of huckleberry for berries.

9. Basecoat mittens with clay bisque. Shade with burnt umber. Paint stripes with green umber.

10. Paint coal buttons on snowman with pure black.

Snow on Card & Envelope:

1. Basecoat with warm white.

2. Shade with burnt carmine.

Bird on Envelope:

Paint same as bird on snowman's hat.

Background:

Shade around edges of card and around lower left corner of envelope with Burnt Umber. Let dry.

FINISH

1. Add linework details and outlines with the black pen.

2. Spatter all surfaces with wicker white, using toothbrush.

3. Cut out snowman ornament. Use the black pen to write a message or verse on the back or simply date it as a keepsake.

4. Cut a 7" piece of linen string. Tie ends together in a knot. Glue on back of ornament.

5. Cut a small piece of mounting tape. Attach ornament to card with tape. Press firmly to hold in place.

TIP: Position mounting tape so that you can tuck the linen string on the tape so the string won't be visible on the card. ❏

Envelope

PATTERNS
(actual size)

Card

Ornament

Merry Christmas Tree

By Marci Donley

Embossed stamping and traditional colors create a beautiful holiday card.

SUPPLIES

Paper:

Red card, 4-1/4" x 5-1/2"
(1/2 sheet of card stock)

White glossy card stock, 4-1/2" square

Green shiny paper 3-3/4" x 5"

Mulberry, rice, or other lacy paper

Tools & Other Supplies:

Decorative edge scissors

Stamps - Christmas tree, Merry
Christmas square, holiday greeting

Pigment inks - Red, green

Embossing pen

Embossing powders - Gold, clear
sparkle, and white

Heat tool

Green tassel

Glue

Hole punch, 1/8"

INSTRUCTIONS

EMBOSS

1. Stamp the tree on white glossy paper with green ink. Stamp the Merry Christmas square with red ink, placing it so it looks like the stand for the tree. Emboss with clear sparkle powder.

2. Use the embossing pen to draw the garland flourish over the tree. Emboss with gold powder.

3. Stamp the message inside the card. Emboss with white powder.

4. Stamp the Merry Christmas square on the envelope with red and green inks.

ASSEMBLE

1. Trim around the tree with the decorative scissors.

2. Adhere to the card in this order: Green paper, lacy paper, and tree.

3. Punch the left side of the card and add a tassel. Secure the end knot with glue. ❏

Wynter Thyme Blessings

By Marnie Lyn Adams

SUPPLIES

Paper:

140 lb. soft press watercolor paper, 8-1/2" x 11" (Hot press paper may be substituted.)

Watercolor Pencils:

Black

Cool grey

Copenhagen

Cream

Crimson red

Dark green

Dark brown

Dark umber

French grey

Grass green

Spanish orange

Terra cotta

Ultramarine

Tools & Other Supplies:

Black permanent ink pens - 03, 05, 08

Paint brush - #6 round

Graphite transfer paper

Kneaded eraser

Pencil & sharpener

Ruler

Paper towels

Water container

Tracing paper

INSTRUCTIONS

PREPARE

1. Fold the watercolor paper to create a vertical card 5-1/2" x 8-1/2".
2. Trace pattern. Using graphite paper, transfer pattern to front of card. Use kneaded eraser to erase any mistakes.

INK

1. Using the 03 pen, ink the hat band details, the scarf details, and the patch details.
2. Using the 08 pen, ink the lettering, the dots, and the patch and border outlines.
3. Using the 05 pen, ink the remaining lines.

COLOR THE DESIGN

Use the photo as a guide.

1. With cream, color the heart patches.
2. With spanish orange, color the stars and the carrot nose.
3. With french grey, color the ground.
4. With cool grey, color the patches with * marks.
5. With crimson red, color the birds and the dot patches.
6. With terra cotta, color the hearts, the birds' wings, and the ticking patches.
7. With ultramarine, color the dotted squares on the hat band, half the stripes on the scarf, and the dotted stripe patches.
8. With copenhagen, color the sky and the flower patches.
9. With grass green, color the diagonal patches.
10. With dark green, color the solid squares on the hat band, half the stripes on the scarf, and the circle patches.
11. With dark umber, color the sign, the button on the hat, and the squiggle patches.
12. With dark brown, color the hat, the button on the large heart, and the patches with # markings.
13. With black, color the snowman's eyes, mouth, and buttons.

PATTERN

Enlarge at 125% for actual size

BRUSH

Wet colored areas with #6 brush dampened with water. Hint: every time the brush is put in water, blot on a paper towel, and rinse thoroughly between colors. Allow to dry overnight. ❑

Warm Winter Wishes

By Marnie Lyn Adams

SUPPLIES

Paper:

140 lb. cold press watercolor paper, 8-1/2" x 11"

Acrylic Craft Paints:

Antique white	Antique gold
Barn red	Black
Brown oxide	Dusty mauve
Flesh	Hunter green
Ivory	Kelly green
Liberty blue	Midnight blue
Military blue	Tapestry wine
Vineyard green	

Colored Pencils:

Black	Copenhagen blue
Olive green	Terra cotta
White	

Tools & Other Supplies:

Black permanent ink pens - 05, 08

Paint brushes - #2 round, #6 round

Wet palette or disposable foam plate

Graphite paper

Kneaded eraser

Pencil & sharpener

Ruler

Paper towels

Water container

Tracing paper

INSTRUCTIONS

PREPARE

1. Fold the watercolor paper to create a vertical card 5-1/2" x 8-1/2".

2. Trace pattern. Using graphite paper, transfer pattern to front of card. Use kneaded eraser to erase any mistakes.

PAINT THE DESIGN

See the project photo as a guide; use the #2 brush for more detailed areas and #6 brush for larger areas. Several coats may be necessary; complete one coat over the entire design and allow to dry before painting the next coat.

1. With liberty blue, paint the left side, the block behind the snowman, the block behind the holly leaf, the block behind the candy cane, and the block behind the bottom button.

2. With kelly green, paint the right side, the block behind Santa, the block behind the ornament, the block behind the mitten, and the block behind the left button.

3. With dusty mauve, paint the block behind the lettering, the block behind the star, the block behind the stocking, the block behind the right button, the block behind the heart, and Santa's nose.

4. With antique white, paint the snowman's face, Santa's hair and beard, the left button on Santa's hat, the block behind the Christmas tree, the top of the ornament, the candy cane, and the left and right buttons.

5. With ivory, paint the top of the snowman's hat, Santa's hat, the mitten cuff, the stocking cuff, the block behind the moon, the middle and right buttons on santa's hat, and the bottom button.

6. With antique gold, paint the inner border, the moon, the star, and the carrot nose.

7. With flesh, paint Santa's face.

8. With vineyard green, paint the snowman's hat cuff, the snowman's scarf, the holly leaf, the Christmas tree, and one-third of the snowman's hat pom pom.

9. With barn red, paint Santa's hat cuff and ball, the mitten, the candy cane stripes, and one-third of the snowman's hat pom pom.

10. With military blue, paint the snowman's hat patch, the ornament, the stocking, and one-third of the snowman's hat pom pom.

11. With brown oxide, paint the heart and the Christmas tree trunk.

12. With black, paint the snowman's eyes and mouth and Santa's eyes.

13. With brown oxide, barn red, tapestry wine, military blue, midnight blue, vineyard green, and hunter green, randomly paint solid border patches. Allow to dry overnight.

INK

1. *Option:* Use graphite paper to transfer the lettering. TIP: Cut the lettering block from the paper pattern. Position and transfer.

2. Using the 05 pen, ink the border, border designs, and the stitches on the hat patch.

3. Using the 08 pen, ink Santa, the snowman, the buttonholes, and the lettering.

COLOR WITH PENCILS

1. With the Copenhagen blue pencil, add dots to the snowman's hat, and stripes and fringe to the snowman's scarf.

2. With the terra cotta pencil, add dots to the snowman's hat, Xs on the hat patch, stripes to Santa's hat, and Santa's cheeks.

3. With the olive green pencil, add dots to the snowman's hat.

4. With the black pencil, add details to the buttons and stitch lines to the border.

5. With the white pencil, add stripes to the snowman's scarf, stripes on the inner border, snowflakes and dots to the left side, and swirls and dots to the right side. ❑

Pattern on page 120

PATTERN

Enlarge at 125%
for actual size

*Instructions on
page 119*

PATTERN

(actual size)

*Instructions on
page 121*

Some Assembly Required

By Marnie Lyn Adams

SUPPLIES

Paper:

140 lb. cold press watercolor paper, 8-1/2" x 5-1/2"

Acrylic Gouache:

Brown earth

Carbon black

Warm white

Acrylic Craft Paints:

Cornflower

Geranium

Marigold

Vines

Tools & Other Supplies:

Black permanent ink pen - 05

Paint brushes - #2 round, 3/4" wash

Wet palette or disposable foam plate

Graphite paper

Kneaded eraser

Pencil & sharpener

Ruler

Paper towels

Water container

Tracing paper

INSTRUCTIONS

PREPARE

1. Fold the watercolor paper to create a vertical card 4-1/4" x 5-1/2".

2. Using the 3/4" brush with cornflower, paint the background. Allow to dry for several hours.

3. Trace pattern. Using graphite paper, transfer pattern to front of card. Use kneaded eraser to erase any mistakes.

PAINT THE DESIGN

Use the #2 brush and the photo as a guide.

1. With brown earth, paint the two sticks.

2. With geranium, paint the hat patch, the top stripe of the scarf, and the right button.

3. With vines, paint the hat sash and middle stripe of the scarf.

4. With marigold, paint the carrot nose, the bottom stripe of the scarf, and the left button.

5. With carbon black, paint the hat, the vertical stripes of the scarf, and the coal eyes and mouth.

6. With warm white, paint the snowman and snowflakes. Allow paint to dry overnight.

INK

Ink the entire design. ❑

Holiday Home

By Marnie Lyn Adams

SUPPLIES

Paper:

140 lb. soft press watercolor paper, 8-1/2" x 5-1/2" (Hot press watercolor paper may be substituted.)

Watercolor Pencils:

Black

Carmine red

Cool grey

Copenhagen

Crimson red

Dark brown

Dark green

Dark umber

French grey

Grass green

Spanish orange

Sunburst yellow

Ultramarine

Tools & Other Supplies:

Black permanent ink pens - 03, 05, 08

Paint brushes - #2 round, 3/4" wash

10 tea bags (orange pekoe or other black tea)

1 cup water

Graphite paper

Kneaded eraser

Pencil & sharpener

Ruler

Paper towels

Water container

Tracing paper

INSTRUCTIONS

PREPARE

1. Fold the watercolor paper to create a horizontal card 5-1/2" x 4-1/4".
2. Trace the pattern. Using graphite paper, transfer pattern to front of card. Use kneaded eraser to erase any mistakes.

COLOR THE DESIGN

Use the photo as a guide.

1. With sunburst yellow, color the moon and the stars on the tops of the trees.
2. With Spanish orange, color the stars in the background.
3. With French grey, color half the striped squares.
4. With cool grey, color the other half of the striped squares.
5. With carmine red, color half the dotted squares.
6. With crimson red, color the other half of the dotted squares.
7. With Copenhagen, color the sky.
8. With ultramarine, color the house.
9. With dark brown, color the chimney and half the roof tiles.
10. With dark umber, color the tree trunks and the rest of the roof tiles.
11. With grass green, color the middle sections of both trees.
12. With dark green, color the top and bottom sections of both trees.
13. With black, color the windows and door.

BRUSH WITH WATER, THEN TEA

1. Wet colored areas using a #2 brush dampened with water. TIP: Every time you put the brush in water, blot it on a paper towel. Rinse thoroughly between colors.
2. To make tea stain, heat water on the stove or in a microwave oven. Add teabags to water and steep 30 minutes. Remove teabags.
3. Use a 3/4" brush to apply the tea stain for an antique look. Allow to dry for several hours.
4. Apply a second coat of tea. Allow to dry overnight.

INK

1. Using the 03 pen, ink the thin vertical lines.
2. Using the 08 pen, ink the stars, star dots, moon, moon dots, trees, house, and oval border.
3. Using the 05 pen, ink the small dots. ❑

PATTERN

(actual size)

Christmas Poinsettia

By Dolores Lennon

SUPPLIES

Paper:

140 lb. cold press watercolor paper postcard

Acrylic Craft Paints:

Calico red

Clover

Holiday red

Thicket

Tools & Other Supplies:

Paint brush - #8 round

Black permanent ink pen, 005

Paper towels

Gray transfer paper & stylus

Tracing paper & pencil

Waxed paper palette

2 water containers (one for clean water, one for rinsing)

INSTRUCTIONS

PREPARE

1. Trace pattern and transfer design.

2. Ink the design and write a message.

3. Make washes (water + a touch of paint) of each color.

PAINT THE DESIGN

Use the examples on the Poinsettia Worksheet as guides.

1. Dampen each petal with clean water.

2. Apply a wash of either calico red or holiday red to each petal, starting with every other petal so that color doesn't run. Let dry. (Fig. 1)

3. Complete the remaining petals. (Fig. 1) Let dry.

4. Dampen petals with clean water.

5. Add a deeper, darker wash of holiday red, working from the petal's center outward. (Fig. 2)

6. Apply a wash of clover to the center. (Fig. 2)

7. Apply a thin wash of either clover or thicket to each leaf. (Fig. 2)

8. Add a holiday red wash to some leaf edges. (Fig. 2) ❑

Poinsettia Worksheet

Fig. 1

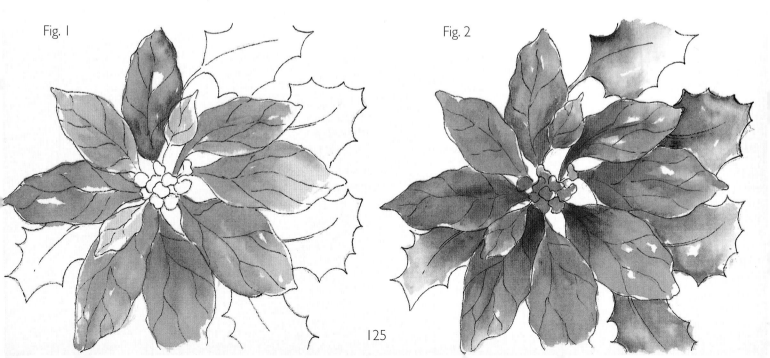

Fig. 2

Happy New Year

By Marci Donley

This card has a photo collage with a craft foam frame that's decorated with dimensional paper paint. TIP: Use a piece of scrap paper to practice writing with paint.

SUPPLIES

Paper:

Black card stock, 6" x 12"

Several color photos

Plain paper, 5-1/2" square

Tools & Other Supplies:

Dimensional paper paint -
  Clear glitter, tapioca

Red craft foam, 6" square

Tracing paper

Craft knife

Ruler

Glue

INSTRUCTIONS

MAKE THE COLLAGE

1. Fold the black card stock to form a 6" square card.

2. Trim the photos to different sizes for the collage.

3. Arrange the photos on the 5-1/2" paper square. Glue them in place.

ASSEMBLE

1. Glue the photo collage to the front of the card.

2. Cut a piece of craft foam 5-7/8" square. Measure in 1/2" from all sides and cut out the center to make the frame. Cut out a small square of foam to decorate the envelope.

3. Place the tracing paper over the foam frame. Write your message on the tracing paper to make sure they fit and are positioned as you wish. When you are happy with the placement, use the tracing paper as a guide and write the words lightly in pencil on the foam.

4. Write with tapioca paper paint over the penciled letters. Decorate the corners and the foam square for the envelope with clear glitter paint. Let dry.

5. Glue the frame to the card front over the photo collage. Glue the foam square to the envelope. ❏

Metric Conversion Chart

Inches to Millimeters and Centimeters

Inches	MM	CM	Inches	MM	CM
1/8	3	.3	2	51	5.1
1/4	6	.6	3	76	7.6
3/8	10	1.0	4	102	10.2
1/2	13	1.3	5	127	12.7
5/8	16	1.6	6	152	15.2
3/4	19	1.9	7	178	17.8
7/8	22	2.2	8	203	20.3
1	25	2.5	9	229	22.9
1-1/4	32	3.2	10	254	25.4
1-1/2	38	3.8	11	279	27.9
1-3/4	44	4.4	12	305	30.5

Yards to Meters

Yards	Meters	Yards	Meters
1/8	.11	2	1.83
1/4	.23	3	2.74
3/8	.34	4	3.66
1/2	.46	5	4.57
5/8	.57	6	5.49
3/4	.69	7	6.40
7/8	.80	8	7.32
1	.91	9	8.23
		10	9.14

Index